Tending the Valley

Tending the Valley

A Prairie Restoration Odyssey

Alice D'Alessio

WISCONSIN HISTORICAL SOCIETY PRESS

Published by the Wisconsin Historical Society Press
Publishers since 1855

The Wisconsin Historical Society helps people connect to the past by collecting, preserving, and sharing stories. Founded in 1846, the Society is one of the nation's finest historical institutions.
Join the Wisconsin Historical Society: wisconsinhistory.org/membership

The front cover painting *Alice Searching* by artist Dagny Myrah depicts author Alice D'Alessio walking on her family's Ridgeway valley land.

Interior drawings are by Gary Cox, Cox and Co. The map on page 33 is by Alice D'Alessio.

A portion of this book's proceeds will benefit the Driftless Area Land Conservancy.

Printed in Wisconsin, USA
Cover design and book composition by Wendy Holdman

24 23 22 21 20   1 2 3 4 5

Library of Congress Cataloging-in-Publication Data
Names: D'Alessio, Alice, author.
Title: Tending the valley: a prairie restoration odyssey / Alice D'Alessio.
Description: Madison : Wisconsin Historical Society Press, 2020.
Identifiers: LCCN 2020018574 (print) | LCCN 2020018575 (e-book) |
    ISBN 9780870209505 (paperback) | ISBN 9780870209512 (e-book)
Subjects: LCSH: Prairie restoration—Wisconsin—Biography. | Restoration
    ecology—Wisconsin—Biography.
Classification: LCC QH105.W6 D34 2020 (print) | LCC QH105.W6 (e-book) |
    DDC 333.74/15309775—dc23
LC record available at https://lccn.loc.gov/2020018574
LC e-book record available at https://lccn.loc.gov/2020018575

♾ The paper used in this publication meets the minimum requirements of the American National Standard for Information Sciences—Permanence of Paper for Printed Library Materials, ANSI Z39.48–1992.

Inventory

How we dug in fifteen logs for steps
to carry us up the back hill
to the farmer's fence,
named it Sunset Boulevard
put a bench there facing west;

How we tried to make a prairie—
burning, lugging eighteen buckets of seed
and flinging in wide arcs till we ached
and dropped, tired and groaning on the deck,
and watched five crows
pick out their favorites. How on our knees
we cheered the ruddy clumps of bluestem,
the first three stalks of Indian Plantain,
Compass Plant. It takes a thousand years
to make a prairie, but we could tell ourselves
this was the start.

How we watch some hundred billion stars
slide left to right each night
while coyotes harmonize
and bats dip and swoop
in their nightly smorgasbord.

We'll be old here, perhaps next year,
and maybe the world will fracture—
sluff away under the weight of its sorrows—
but you and I have counted these moments
balanced the tally, and called ourselves rich.

—ALICE D'ALESSIO, DAYS WE ARE GIVEN,
EARTH'S DAUGHTERS PRESS, 2006

Contents

Prologue

About fifteen or twenty miles west of Madison, Wisconsin, the hills are steeper and the valleys narrow, as though somebody took the map and crumpled it in a fist to create a more interesting landscape. It's known as the Driftless Area. The glacier that scraped and flattened the rest of Wisconsin missed the southwest corner, leaving a rugged landscape ribboned with meandering streams and roads, still forested in places and stacked with sandstone cliffs and outcroppings.

Here in early 1960, John and Sally Marshall found a hidden valley, pooled with mist, patchy with wildflowers, surrounded by high wooded hills. Since reading Aldo Leopold, they had been looking for some wilderness land and were particularly attracted to the Driftless Area. They heard about land owned by an elderly woman named Henrietta Reese Cross, who had inherited forty acres of an eighty-acre valley from her father. Enchanted by what they found there, they visited Mrs. Cross in her small home in Ridgeway and offered to buy the land, but she was reluctant to sell. They visited her several times, the last time in 1961 in a nursing home. Finally she agreed to sell them the forty acres if they promised to take care of the land and not divide it up and sell it to a developer. The Marshalls later bought an additional forty acres and then another thirty-five, for a total of one hundred and fifteen.

Several friends of the Marshalls had also bought property in the area, and John and Sally enjoyed picnicking with them, hiking, climbing, and discovering. The adjacent landowner was a hydrologist and helped John design a dam in the stream to create a fishpond. They received approval from the Wisconsin

Department of Natural Resources, and for a number of years John enjoyed his pond, until the muskrats dug holes in the dam.

Sally was more interested in the plants and kept lists of the various wildflowers. Together they set about cleaning up an old rustic farmhouse on the property to provide sleeping space and hired a carpenter to construct an addition: a large deck in the front of the cabin looking out over the spectacular view and a small bunkroom with a basement below.

The Marshalls' three children, Jan, Laird, and Owen, were in college or traveling, but they visited their parents in the valley occasionally. Jan and her husband bought nearby land in Ridgeway as well. When John and Sally died, the land was passed on to the three, who continued to visit from time to time to picnic with friends, to hike, or to explore. Most of the time, hunters, coyotes, birds, field mice, and invasive plants claimed the place as their own.

This is the story of what came next: of the people who loved the land and who worked hard to restore it to its natural state, before it had been mined and farmed and grazed. Over the course of thirty years, they learned much, enjoyed successes, suffered disappointments. And still, they remained in awe, despairing and delighting at nature's surprises.

Discovery

Maybe just looking and listening is the real work. Maybe the world, without us, is the real poem.

—MARY OLIVER, *THE LEAF AND THE CLOUD*

Arrival

I remember the first day I saw the valley in May 1983. It was gray and drizzly when my newfound partner, Laird Marshall, drove me down the long, rutted driveway, creeping slowly around the steep hairpin turns in his rattly old Volvo. When we had met several months before, he told me about the wilderness land that his parents had owned and left to him and his siblings.

I was eager to see it, and he had chosen a Sunday, when neither of us was working. He had invited his cousin David Hamel and David's wife, Shelley—the couple who had introduced us some months earlier—to come with us that day, for what was billed as a picnic.

The driveway—more like a path—sloped between high, thickly wooded ridges and outcroppings of sandstone. We emerged from a tunnel of woods beside a shabby gray shack. Wood-sided, paint-peeling, it was shuttered and forlorn. A large roofed deck jutted out in front, and we climbed the three sagging steps to this platform and turned to look toward the open fields and the ridges that surrounded them. Like a door opening, or curtains being pulled back, the valley unfolded. I know I felt the same mixture of awe and delight that I have felt each time in the thirty-plus years that I've climbed the steps and made that slow, half-circle turn.

Whatever the season, the impact is the same: an expanse of

field—maybe fifteen acres—always changing. Spring green to summer yellow-gold, autumn tawny to winter white, then March's discouraging brown again restarting the cycle. It's a patchwork of black after a burn, and then suddenly new bright green, and on into a multicolored summer and the festive streamers of fall.

Steep hillsides, thick with pine, oak, hickory, and walnut, rise above the field on all sides. And over all, the wide-open sky stretches like an immense canvas, waiting for the watercolor fantasies that will play across it during the day, or the saucer-sized stars that appear in the blue-black night. The distance is so varied, so beautifully framed in ridges and dark pine fringe, that it compels you to gaze, and gaze long.

That May day we wandered over much of the 115 acres—up and down hills and through woods that were tangled and overgrown with bramble in places, wet and uninviting. David and Shelley had visited the valley before and were eager to show us some of their favorite areas. I was particularly enchanted with the rock outcroppings, layered in soft colors, lichened and crumbling. Foxes lived there. We could see their scat and smell their musky odor.

We visited the old fishing pond that Laird's parents had established. Muskrats had tunneled through the dam, and the pond had emptied and grown over with reed canary grass. Elsewhere along the stream we discovered beaver dams. These would come and go over the years—now in one spot, now another.

At the end of our rambles, when the rain became more persistent, we returned to the deck for shelter and from there ventured inside the cabin. I think the door wasn't locked, or if it was, David forced the lock on the rotting doorjamb to get in, where we made a different kind of discovery.

The cabin had been neglected for years. Deer hunters had made themselves at home in the basement, which was a cement block room under the small bunkroom, all part of Laird's parents' addition. It was dark and damp, with seepage from the back wall

and mouse droppings everywhere. Dirty frying pans and dishes added to the smell. It was the sort of space that made you want to escape immediately.

A spiral staircase built around a massive trunk of a red pine led upstairs to the small bunkroom, consisting of two double-decker platforms piled with narrow mattresses. Once again, the smell of mildew and rot, of dank, unstirred air, was nearly suffocating.

For many people, the condition of the cabin could have been enough to quell the excitement of the day. But I was raised with brothers and spent my summers on an uncle's farm with four boy cousins. Scruffy, barefoot, and curious, we slept in the barn, explored caves, scaled trees, and wallowed in swimming holes. At night, we bunked down in flour-sack sheets that were always gritty with sand. I never learned what squeamish was. This cabin, to me, was just another adventure.

A narrow hallway led from the newer area to the original cabin. Probably more than a hundred years old, it had once been a three-room farmhouse, but the walls had been knocked out to create one space, approximately nineteen by thirteen feet in size. An ancient wood cookstove squatted in the middle of the remaining space. The back area was jammed with a workbench and a vast collection of rusty tools and hardware.

Here the condition of the interior was just as appalling, though with the large front shutters removed, the space was at least light.

Laird's parents had been dead for more than a decade and the cabin more or less abandoned. They had apparently used this area as sleeping quarters and had built in a linen closet and two wooden bunks. The closet stood open, providing comfortable quarters for countless generations of mice; sheets and towels in various stages of gnawed-ness hung out of shelves or lay fallen to the floor. Old newspapers and magazines also littered the floor. The walls had been plaster, painted a rosy pink. The plaster was crumbling off in places, adding to the debris on the floor and making it difficult to take even the few steps necessary to view the wreckage.

And yet, in the midst of the disorder, the smell and the aura of hopeless abandon, I sensed the promise. The windows framed the view—wild, varied, and intriguing. We could wake to a ridgetop horizon of white pines. The sun would ease above them and slant into this window.

On that first day we closed up the shutters and left, returning to our entanglements in Madison: the challenge of a new job, my still-new relationship with Laird, the winding down of my worn-out marriage, the reality of my two older sons' college graduation, departure of my younger son for a year in India, and the sale of the house I had lived in for seventeen years.

Those months in 1983 and 1984 and were so layered with loss and renewal, endings and beginnings, that I was too distracted to recognize that a small, tenacious seed had been planted in my subconscious. Like the seed of the graceful big bluestem, it would grow very slowly, invisible for the first year as it concentrated its life force on sinking its roots. And it sank its roots deep.

Looking and Listening

At first, just knowing the valley was enough. As my relationship with Laird grew, we visited more often, learning and naming the varied flora, delighting in finding caves and grottoes. David and Shelley were also enthralled with the valley and often initiated a visit—to see what was happening, to explore, and to discover. We reveled in the sweaty exertion of climbing higher and higher through the tallest pines, scaling the sandstone cliffs on which they clung, and sitting there on top, among the wild huckleberry and pipsissewa. Velvet mosses cushioned us, soft and damp, and lichen adorned the rocks like green lace. We listened to the hushed sough in the pine tops. That was enough.

By 1985, we visited almost every weekend. When I wasn't there, the valley existed in my imagination—my own green garden, waiting for me to re-enter its paths when I needed comfort from my other life. For ten or more years after discovering the valley, I was working in Madison as a corporate communications director for a large firm—the lone woman in a male-dominated world. The work was stressful, and I needed respite. Since the valley was only about thirty-five miles from Madison, sometimes Laird would pick me up from work and we'd drive to the valley for a quiet picnic, sitting in rickety chairs on the old deck—me in my business suit and heels recounting my day, gaining small teaspoons of peace to sustain me for a few more days and weeks.

Once he picked me up directly from the airport, having packed my jeans and boots, a cooler of drinks, and dinner. Away from the demands of the workplace, I could relax in the sweet harmony of our hiding place.

David and Shelley were ideal co-discoverers, and their delight equaled and intensified ours. Curious and observant, brimming with ideas and speculations, they shared our early years of learning and laboring.

We picnicked on Wave Point, so named by Shelley because she was sure the giant boulders were carved with the watermarks of prehistoric waves. Laird and I discovered another high ridge where a bowl-shaped grotto among the tall trees led to an abrupt cliff rise, and the dripping cliffs were festooned with ferns in many varieties and sizes. We couldn't wait to take David and Shelley to our new find, which Laird immediately named "The Grotto of Our Lady of Perpetual Tears." Shelley returned with a fern book and identified the many varieties of ferns.

We learned the different milkweeds and blew their delicate seed hairs on the wind. We found a tall, fringed orchid along the stream—like a two-foot tall wand, tied with purple-winged ribbons. We found nodding trillium and masses of shooting stars in the woods. Marsh marigolds were baskets of gold in the marshy areas; on the dry hillsides, puccoons echoed the same intense color with their flat, five-petaled faces.

Some nights we crept on tiptoe down to the stream, where the beavers were constructing murky ponds. By moonlight we could watch these small, sleek engineers as they circled and gnawed small willows, nudged them into place, and caulked them with mud, following some preordained design.

We often slept outside, unrolling our sleeping bags on the weathered deck. In the spring, we listened for spring peepers, chorus frogs, leopard frogs, and finally the banjo twang of the bull frog. Always, the whip-poor-will would begin his chant at a quarter past nine in the evening. And all night, the barred owl hooted, sometimes stirring up a dialogue back and forth with friends or enemies. Across the prairie and up the hill, a chorus of coyotes would sing from time to time. At first light, the joyful, exuberant discordance of the bird chorus reminded me of a symphony orchestra tuning up.

In the early days, we casually scattered big bluestem seed among the goldenrod stalks that dominated the valley fields, hoping to rejuvenate the prairie. We read about the Midwest prairies that early settlers described. And then one day as we looked out across our field, we dreamed a prairie that was gone. This green and golden, thistle-dotted, butterfly-speckled field was not enough. We wanted that prairie back.

From then on, our relationship with the valley began to change, slowly and imperceptibly at first. It wasn't there just to look at. It was no longer simply a tranquil retreat, a rustic hideaway for friends to gather and enjoy good food and drinks on the deck, and perhaps take a grudging stroll to look for beaver dams, wildflowers, or morels. Looking and listening were no longer enough. At least, not for me.

Beginnings

The more we read, the more we learned. The more we learned, the more we felt an obligation to the land. Years before, I had read Aldo Leopold's *A Sand County Almanac*, and now I read it again.

The words of Leopold and of others who have written on land restoration and stewardship stirred me with a passion that changed my life. I became obsessed with returning the valley to its former condition, restoring native species and eradicating exotic or invasive species. I wanted it back the way it was two hundred years ago, before the lead miners burrowed tunnels, before the wheat and cornfields smothered the prairie, before the sheep and cattle grazed off the trillium and orchids and spiderwort.

David and Shelley were equally enthusiastic, while Laird was a willing partner but not as obsessive. The undertaking we proposed was, of course, more daunting than I imagined. Aldo Leopold made it sound so easy, but he had had sturdy children and graduate students to help him. It would certainly have helped if one of us had a degree in botany, rather than English literature and mathematics. One of my friends pointed out that, at an acre a year, our quixotic mission would take us 115 years. Nor could I garner wholehearted enthusiasm from among my closest friends and relatives.

"I don't like to come out any more because you're always

working," said Laird's sister, Jan. "It looks pretty and green from up here on the deck. Why don't you just let it alone?"

"Box elder trees are pretty too," said his sister-in-law, Meg. "Anyhow, why do you want a prairie? Just let natural succession take place."

Even Laird, although he subscribed to the principles of restoration, admitted that he would rather sit on the deck and read than tackle an acre of honeysuckle.

While I could understand their reluctance, I couldn't let it go. How can anyone explain obsession? Why is it a thrill to see how the little bluestem has thickened into a tawny blanket on the dry prairie? How it creates a rippling backdrop for the tiny harebells, the downy gentians, and liatris (blazing star) that become more abundant with each spring burn? I don't know. I can't pretend it's instinct; I'm not like the phoebe who comes back to rebuild her nest under the deck—even though she gets disturbed and routed so often. But I do try to understand why restoration ecology is so important to me. Perhaps it's because I have control over so little in the world.

When I descend to this narrow niche of land, wrapped in fog and ridges, where hummingbirds dart and coyotes sing, I feel protected from ill-planned housing developments, draining of wetlands and increasing traffic; from clear-cutting, mining, and pesticides. Here, we could make a small difference.

In the beginning, there was so much we didn't know. But we asked questions, attended workshops, invited out naturalists— botanists, foresters, and restoration specialists—from the Nature Conservancy, the Wisconsin Department of Natural Resources (DNR), and the University of Wisconsin. We picked their brains and took notes and compared notes with David and Shelley. We bought handbooks, workbooks, guidebooks, and identification books. We had to have them all. I was like a kid who has just discovered baseball cards.

We made mistakes. I thought if I liked a plant, all we needed to do was plant it where we thought it ought to be, and it would grow. On the dry prairie, we planted pasqueflower and half a dozen of my favorite, prairie smoke. I fenced them, watered them, crooned to them. And they died. I scattered the seeds of the butterfly weed so beloved of monarch butterflies in an area that seemed ideal, but they never germinated. So I bought butterfly weed in pots, and we planted them, once again fussing and watering, the way I would in my garden at home. I pictured their bright orange July blossoms, swarming with monarchs. Yet my tiny pale green plants with narrow leaves grew spindlier and droopier. Like patients with terminal disease, they finally shriveled away completely.

Laird and I bought ten Turk's-cap lilies to plant along the stream, and we even went so far as to fashion little wire cages to keep rodents from digging them up. We buried them as tenderly as the family jewels in the moist earth, close, but not too close to the willful stream. We never got even one bloom. Oh yes— years later several Turk's-cap lilies appeared magically along the path, far from where we'd buried our bulbs. If plants could thumb their noses, this would be the gesture.

Turk's-cap lily

One truth became clear: we were not in charge. There is a very complex interrelation among prairie plants and between plants and soil. So many variables— climate, microorganisms, deer, insects—were beyond our control. Each year, whether we had tinkered or not, the plant patterns would change. One year we would have a massive bloom of daisy fleabane, which I knew was a noxious weed, and I would despair. The next year it would be gone.

Burning was the one tool about which everyone seemed to agree. I was introduced to the writings of John Curtis, professor of botany and a pioneer of restoration ecology at the University of Wisconsin. In simple terms, burning a field at the right time sets back the cold-season, or invasive, grasses and plants and gives the warm-season, or prairie, plants a better chance to compete.

In April of 1989, we organized our first burn. We had helped at burns on other conservancy land, and David and Shelley had even more experience. We called in experts from the DNR. We were well equipped with humidity gauges, flappers and water packs, a drip torch, and rakes. Our trousers were tucked into sturdy boots; we were gloved, hatted, and scarved. We were ever so cautious.

First, we burned a five-foot-wide swath along one edge—the downwind edge—and down both sides, carefully smothering or spraying stray sparks. When we had a U-shaped fire break blackened, we lit a line of fire across the remaining edge and let it burn. With the wind blowing against it, the fire crawled slowly and purposefully down the length of the valley and stopped when it reached the break at the far end. On the way, tall grasses flared up in plumes; thickets would crackle wildly in a sudden firestorm; small pines and blackberry brambles sizzled and crumpled.

Then it was done. The fire left little feathers of lazy smoke, rising in the cooling late afternoon air. Like a blackboard in a classroom, our blank field was ready for us to devise plans, to create something wonderful. I was as exhilarated as a painter with a fresh canvas. It was a totally satisfying experience, and we congratulated ourselves as we rested on the deck, sweaty and sooty, with our cold beers and chili. Of course we didn't talk about the generations of seed from invasive plants that had inevitably survived and would wait their turn underground.

Within two weeks, the field was green, and only a slight smoky smell and some crunching underfoot as we walked into it reminded us that there had been a fire. That summer the field was lusher than before. We searched it for new species, cataloging our discoveries. A swath of liatris at the far end was easily four feet tall—slender spires in fringed fuchsia; Culver's root and mountain mint were thick. Bottle gentians peered out in profusion, each stem crowded with its intense blue blossoms. None of these plants were new, of course, but they were certainly more vigorous.

Still, despite the success of the first fire, it was very obvious that most of the field, even where we had burned, was in goldenrod, sumac, blackberry, cinquefoil, and other less desirable plants. We had made a very small impact. Although we might refer to the fields as "the prairie," no naturalist would dignify it so.

At about this time we stumbled upon an organization called Prairie Enthusiasts. It was a newly formed, loosely organized group of people—some landowners, some not—who were eager to learn more about prairies, how to encourage them, and how to save them from being plowed under. We made friends and attended many of their meetings—learning how much there was to learn!

We had many years of controlled burns ahead, as well as reseeding and mowing sumac and blackberry, uprooting honeysuckle and autumn olive. And there would be many frustrating days when I would want to succumb to that chorus of voices: Why do you bother? What does it matter? Leave it alone.

Early Days at the Cabin

Within the first few months, we cleared out all the debris from the cabin, swept and scrubbed, and made it at least marginally habitable. The downstairs was still dank and uninviting, so we decided that we should concentrate on the upstairs, removing the crumbling plaster in the old farmhouse part and opening it up into one room. We didn't do the big stuff; our talents are more attuned to sweeping and sorting. Laird and I stapled insulation between the studs, before our deer hunters hammered on pine board siding. The deer hunters were guys who loved to do repairs for us in exchange for the one week a year that they got to stay in the cabin and harvest some of the deer overpopulation. David introduced us to them early in our first valley ventures, and they proved over the years to be loyal and invaluable friends. They even built a new outhouse and a tractor shed for our secondhand tractor.

We moved a futon into the cabin, a secondhand table and chairs, a wood-burning stove, and a little gas cookstove that came from some hunter's trailer. Although our cabin was still pretty stark and scruffy, it was at least tolerable, and we could cook and stay warm. For about twelve years, that was the way the cabin was. We came out frequently on weekends and sometimes during the week as well, since the valley was only a thirty-five-minute drive from our Madison home at the time.

At first, life was very elemental. Each need was satisfied

through a solution more labor-intensive, basic, or primitive than at home. The cabin had no electricity and no running water. When we woke, the first trip was to the new outhouse. A simple enough building, it was constructed of cedar with a screened open space at the top for air circulation. The seat was loose and slid around, and spider webs collected in the corners and under the seat. When I was younger, someone had told me that a vicious kind of spider can live under outhouse seats. Is it the brown recluse? Many people I know might find this all too daunting to face. And I didn't linger.

A roll of toilet paper in a coffee can completed the amenities. No flush handle to take it all away. No chenille seat cover and matching rug, no pristine wash basin, prim curtains, soap dispenser, mirror. By the time we walked back to the cabin our feet were soaked from the morning dew—which is why we ordinarily made this trip in our rubber boots.

If we had slept on the deck, which we almost always did, we stowed the bedding in the storage trunk and hauled the shabby mattresses back inside to stack on the bunks. When we first started using the cabin, I found a mouse family—babies the size of pink cherry tomatoes—in the bottom of the old wooden trunk that Laird's parents had left behind. Nearly all the bedding had nibble holes from those days. I tried putting mothballs in amongst the bedding, but they nearly asphyxiated us. Then I rubbed the trunk edges with oil of peppermint, which someone suggested as a repellent. I never noticed that it repelled anything, but it left a pleasant lingering fragrance. Then we bought a metal trunk. Problem solved.

For breakfast, I would fill the blue enamelware kettle from a jug of water we brought from home. The mice had taken to building nests in the pump, so we didn't use pump water for drinking. I clicked the igniter over the grungy, three-burner propane stove, and, usually, it lit. We had a Chemex drip coffeepot that my son Mark had given us when we first started coming here—and it brewed much better coffee than our ninety-five-dollar Cuisinart at home.

We ate on the deck. David had bought us a large picnic table, which has served us well for many years. If it was after eight in the morning in the summer, the sun had lifted above Lookout Point and was blasting us in the face. Depending on the heat, we either moved the table or put on sunglasses. We munched happily in the warmth, looking out, always looking out. Space is what is so breathtaking in the valley. We took in the far hills, the ragged tree line, and the immense field between, in its many changing colors. Then and always, we are lifted into the space, into and out of ourselves; we float in a languid tranquility that is constantly renewed and renewing. We watched the birds that landed on nearby branches, trying to remember their names, trying to think of new ways to say, "I love this place" and "We are so lucky." And since there weren't many new ways to say it, we said it often.

After breakfast, there were small, comfortable things to be done—folding the sheets, washing the dishes—and we did them in turn, sometimes one of us, sometimes the other, without discussion, without direction. These were simple and repetitive actions that required no deep thought, freeing the mind to meander into other alleyways, lofting into the possibilities that surrounded us. I might have speculated on how the cabin would be different if improved: Would running water make us happier? Would electricity?

I pumped water into the battered black kettle, straining out mouse debris if any. The thirty-year-old pump was rusty and sang a squawking complaint. It took twelve strokes of the handle to bring up the water and many more to fill the kettle. I heated the water on the stove for washing while stacking dishes on the sides of my outdoor sink behind the cabin. It was an ancient, double porcelain sink on wobbly table legs. In between visits, we kept it covered with a blue plastic cover to keep out most of the spiders, leaves, and other debris that wanted to accumulate.

This was one of my favorite places to be. The glaring sunshine of the deck was filtered back here, so it was shady in the morning. Behind me the hillside rose, wooded with maple, oak, and hickory, thick with underbrush. The phoebe nested under the eaves, above the rotting doors that leaned against the house. She would leave in a flurry when I started setting up my "kitchen." I washed dishes in scalding soapy water, then rinsed and stacked them in the dish drainer. My imagination wandered indolently, creating no great ideas, generating only potential chores for the day. When I was done I simply tossed the dishwater into the woods. It was a pretty simple operation, didn't require a septic system, didn't pollute, erode, or cost. It might coat the grasses with unwelcome grease and suds, but I never detected any environmental degradation. The dishes dried in the sun, requiring no energy but that.

The back door to the old house sagged. The screen door, painted many years before by Laird's parents in a royal blue, was cut purposely crooked to fit the crooked doorway, and it was gnawed from the bottom in a jagged hole two or three inches high—maybe by a squirrel who got in somehow and couldn't get out again. Below the door, the sill was rotted away. The deer hunters nailed a board along the bottom of the screen door to close the gap, but an enterprising mouse could easily squeeze in when the heavy outer door was open. Or perhaps even when it was closed. I stacked bricks to disguise what could be an enticing mouse entrance. When stepped on barefoot, dead bees go crunch. A dead mouse in your work boot is even more unsettling.

Several hours after we rose, dew still hung on every leaf and twig, so the greenery in front of the cabin sparkled; an indigo bunting perched in the willow bush and made his chattery announcement, ending emphatically, "sweet-sweet." To the right, the insistent yellow-throated warbler fired back his "witchety-witchety." Up behind the outhouse a towhee chimed in with his three-note statement. Bird-watching purists who scoff at anthro-pomorphizing their calls might resent my saying it sounded very much like "Drink your te-e-e-a." But it did. Although sometimes he stopped lazily halfway, managing only a "Drink your . . ." before trailing off. Small chitters and musical trills formed a background chorus to my morning chores. An occasional airplane hummed in the distance, echoed by some pesky flies.

By midmorning we were probably involved in one or another of the tasks we'd planned. We were either exploring, gathering watercress from the west branch of the creek, spraying, cutting, or taking photos. I know, because we kept a series of journals, wherein whoever was inspired would add some comments or record thoughts on the day's happenings. In addition to the work, we recorded the many picnics, visitors, burns, parties, and cele-brations, as well as the list of people who participated. But often, the journal was a place for reflection, for trying to capture some of the peace of our languorous days and take it home with us. When I want to return to the simple early days of the valley, I reread entries like this one from July of 1988:

> I come alone on a blessed, peaceful day. Black raspberries along the path are ripe, though small and seedy. Brought book on Frank Lloyd Wright. Quiet and contentment. Shadows lengthen across the valley as the sun slips behind the cabin. At 8:15, the last rim of gold retreats from the gentian triangle upward to the pine hillside. Eight crows flap eastward across the valley, as though headed for Ridgeway and a night on the town.

> The deer comes—only one—and stands in the path by the sumac brush pile staring at me, flicking its long ears. I stare back. We make a truce. He ambles a way down the path, looking back at me from time to time. Then he takes off, bounding toward the stream.

Before the Land Was Ours

Early on in our valley adventures we became curious about its history—who had lived here before Laird's parents, and what had they done to the land? We could guess, based on the fact that when we walked across the major field, we could still detect how the land was striated underfoot with even rows, surely the work of some farmer's plow. Behind the outhouse were the remains of an old barn, or perhaps a shed. The roof had fallen in over the hand-hewn square logs, and it was the resting place for various rusted pieces of equipment: milk cans and barrels, parts of a chicken coop, even some bedsprings. Farther up in deep woods we uncovered what seemed to be the foundation of a bigger house, outlined in stone blocks, with trees growing up inside and no other evidence. I thought about excavating the area but never did.

To begin my research, I studied the land abstract that had come down to us through Laird's parents. It listed all the owners since the US government first sold land in the area in the 1850s. The first deed on this land was dated 1855. At that time, it consisted of two forty-acre parcels, and following the abstract we could see how it had passed from one owner to the next. One parcel had been sold about nine times and the other, twelve. The names Rees, later Reese, and Strutt came up prominently. The final entries listed one parcel owned by John Brunker and one by Henrietta Reese Cross—both deeded to John and Sally Marshall in 1961–62.

But abstracts don't contain enough information, so I visited the Wisconsin Historical Society and found the surveyor's notes on microfiche. Sylvester Sibley surveyed the land in February 1832. In his notes he recorded, "Land rolling and first rate. Thinly timbered with oak until I enter the prairie." By this account, the land fit the description of an oak savanna—once common in this area, now nearly gone. Sibley, the early surveyor, also noted the presence of people whom he called "transient diggers." He probably referred to the Ho-Chunk, who had been mining lead in the area for years, smelting the soft, heavy metal for their own use and later selling it to white settlers for bullets and other needs. It's easy to imagine that some of the bullets were used against the Ho-Chunk as the land was gradually bought or wrested from them, as they were driven away into Iowa and later South Dakota.

What we know of the land after that is pieced together from historical records and word of mouth, from local families who have a long history in the area. By 1850, the area was mostly occupied by settlers of northern European descent—with names such as Porter, Delaney, Morrison, Armstrong, and Brigham. After the lead ran out or was no longer profitable, settlers started growing wheat and other small grains and raised livestock—sheep for wool and, later, dairy cows. First-class cheese and butter factories sprang up, the start of a Driftless dairy tradition that has continued into the present.

The original deed for our land dates to 1855, when it was deeded from "the United States of America to David H. Rees." This appears to be an earlier spelling of Reese, the maiden name of the woman who eventually sold the land to Laird's parents in 1961. The Reese farm was called a "Century Farm" because it was in the Reese family for more than one hundred years.

I have tried to imagine what the valley was like when Henrietta Reese Cross and her family owned it. Perhaps she also discovered the grotto and the pine relict. Did she ride down a bumpy dirt road in a wagon to help her father with the harvest? Who lived in the old farmhouse then? Who built the barn? So many questions that I would never answer!

Launching the Wrens

At first, when we slept outside overnight, I was uneasy. During the day, there was plenty to see and hear. But on moonless nights, a velvet blackness fell over the valley, so thick it caused vertigo. The night was a huge hungry maw that threatened to swallow me. Where did the sky join the land? What were the sounds, the howls and screeches? And worst of all, how could we protect ourselves against trespassers? The cabin had obviously been visited over the years, whether by passing vagrants or opportunistic hunters.

I am blessed or cursed with an active imagination, and on such nights I lay awake many nights listening for footsteps, though who would want to walk down that long driveway in the darkness, I couldn't say. Such irrational thoughts grew out of proportion in the creeping, somber hours between midnight and dawn.

The hours stretched on interminably, finally lightening ever so slightly above the ridge in the east, at which point I would usually doze off. I think Laird never knew that when we talked about sleeping at the valley, one of us was getting little actual sleep.

One weekend I arrived alone, determined to stay by myself and meet my nighttime fears head on. Also, I hoped to be there when the house wrens fledged.

They had made their home in an old canvas army ammunition pack that hung by its strap on one of the pine posts supporting the deck roof. The pine branches had been lopped off, leaving six or eight inches as hanging pegs, and over the years various objects accumulated on the pegs—mostly odd gloves, mittens, and hats. The army pack, now the color of weathered wood, had been there ever since I could remember.

One year the wrens moved in. It was a convenient wren nest, if a little unstable in the wind. The flap at the top was open just enough for a thumb-sized wren to slip into, and a ragged hole halfway down the side made a nice exit—facilitating cleanup. So each spring we watched for the buildup of twigs that signaled another blessed event. One wren—the male?—seemed to do most of the nest building, while his bossy mate sat on a higher pine stub giving continuous instructions. For small birds, they were amazingly vocal. We watched quietly from our mattresses or from the picnic table.

In early June, the wren parents were making regular visits to the canvas nest, with not a peep from a babe. It's very hard to see down into the pack without disturbing birds and nest, but to satisfy our curiosity we did take a flashlight and peer inside

after mama and papa (we named them Jenny and Christopher) had left. Sure enough, in the bottom of the untidy collection of small twigs and bits of fluff, we could see three eggs, about the size of miniature jelly beans.

By the next weekend, the eggs had hatched and the feeding process was in full swing. The parents did not like it when large intruders arrived and filled the space on their deck. They must have decided by now that we were no real threat, but they complained bitterly and loudly—and if someone thoughtlessly pulled up a chair near their home or, worse yet, hung a shirt over a peg above the pack, obscuring the entrance—they issued a barrage of abuse.

In and out they flew endlessly, from six in the morning till dusk, bearing small insects or large twitching caterpillars in the top, and bits of baby detritus out the bottom. When the parents were away, we put our ear up against the pack to hear the faint chip-chipping inside. By the next weekend, the chorus inside had grown louder and more insistent. Each time a parent arrived with a juicy morsel, a whole clamor of excitement shook the gray knapsack. In between feedings we heard the youngsters tussling around in the twigs, scraping their little wire toes on the coarse canvas.

This weekend my solitary presence seemed scarcely noted by the harried parents. Their offspring had matured to rowdy adolescents, rarely still or quiet. They were obviously close to launching, and the parents fussed and fed, chattered and cautioned and advised. A steady supply of large caterpillars was greeted with boisterous chirps.

Now, suddenly, I saw their little gray faces and white beaks framed in the door hole. When I opened the door, they froze—either well trained or reacting on instinct. Next, one fuzzy baby clutched the torn edge of the exit hole and stood up tall to view the outside world. Still holding tight, his tiny black eyes stared out at suddenly larger horizons. How vast and terrifying the world must look to someone raised in the cozy confines of an army ammunition pack! I could see only one baby. Surely one miniature bit of gray fluff couldn't make so much clamor—though we had already figured that 60 percent of wren body weight must be vocal equipment.

The scuffling in the bottom of the pack was now augmented with a whirring sound, and I suspected they were exercising tiny wings in anticipation of their big launch. And their beleaguered parents were probably thinking, "Boy, will I be glad to get them out of the house!"

Friday night, I slept inside, succumbing to timidity. Still, it was a broken and uneasy sleep. In the morning, as I reached the screen door leading out to the deck, I stopped to note a flurry of activity at the wren household. Instead of one wren flying in and out, I saw a cluster of heads. The mother stood on a peg above the nest, while the father arrived to bring last-minute caterpillar provisions, amidst a palpable air of excitement. Three tiny gray faces bobbed and peered out of the hole, chit-chitting in response to their parents' steady stream of admonitions. I stayed at the door, quietly observing this monumental event in the life of the wrenlets: the mother urging and cajoling them to take the next daring step. She flew to the railing, looked back, and took off for the nearest tree. Would they know how to follow her?

The first babe scuttled out, wobbled uncertainly atop the pack, and hopped to a higher pine stub. Then she was gone, so suddenly that I barely saw it happen! Somehow I expected her to flutter to the deck and do some short practice runs, but she was already out in the bushes swelling the chorus.

The next one was a little more timid. He clutched the edge of the fabric, urged on by the third sibling. From his perch on the launching peg, he carried on a long conversation, either with his remaining nest mate or with his parents, waiting anxiously in the cherry tree. "Chitt-chitt," he said, stretching wings the size of Barbie mittens, and "chitt-chitt" replied the last sibling. Suddenly number two took off. Aiming for the deck railing but not gaining enough altitude, he fluttered down the supporting post, bounced off the edge of the deck and disappeared from sight. I was confident that he would recover, take to the air again, and plan his flight pattern a little more prudently. Or else he would be just one tender morsel for a watching owl.

Now only one baby remained—chittering anxiously, teetering at the brink of her debut. She worried a little more, but her course was clear. The nest behind her was quiet and empty, with no place to go but out. The little wings poked out and fluttered experimentally, and with one terrifying leap she was airborne, sailing between deck and rail, and landing on a branch in the dogwood bush by the fire pit. Oh, brave new world of green and sky and countless tidbits to please a wren's gullet!

Thinking of my own restless night, my reluctance to sleep exposed on the deck in the peaceful night, I admired the tiny wrens for the confidence with which they alighted into a potentially dangerous world. In the journal that day, I noted,

> This morning at 7:15 am the baby wrens fledged! I was just inside the screen door quietly witnessing the whole momentous matriculation. Three babes. Out into the world! I try not to think of the many predators that might welcome a tasty wren tidbit! They are certainly much braver than I. Size has little to do with courage!

It was hard to know how much coaching and protection the parents were obliged to provide from there on. Did the family stay together, foraging where the insects were the thickest? Did the parents teach their offspring how to probe under tree bark and scour the undersides of leaves—or was it every wren for himself

or herself from then on? I don't know. The woods are vast and
the birds many. I do know the adults have come back to visit their
nest once or twice. Perhaps they were checking to be sure no
one had been left behind. Or maybe they were simply revisiting
the scene of their most productive activity, feeling suddenly lost,
purposeless, and lonely.

Naming

I love learning the names of things. I love saying the names of plants over and over, tasting the quick Latin syllables on my tongue. The flowers: *Ratibida pinnata* (gray-headed coneflower); the grasses: *Andropogon gerardii* and *Schizachyrium scoparium* (big and little bluestem); and the trees: *Quercus alba* (white oak), *Quercus macrocarpa* (bur oak). In the first few years I was constantly making lists of plants and their date of bloom. At least seventy-five and probably far more different plants bloomed on our land at various times, and we learned (and soon forgot) the Latin names as well as the common. When in doubt, Laird would dub them "starry twinkle" or "false Lucinda's purse" and then check our growing library.

We also named special places in the valley over the years, as a way of reference. Because the lowlands, hillsides, woods, and rock outcroppings sprawl for 115 acres, we needed landmarks to be able to tell each other where we had found a deer carcass, for instance, or where we wanted to go for a picnic. And so we had Piney Point and Lookout Point and Wave Point. At Wet Butte, a friend had sat down to take a thorn from her shoe and ended up with a damp bottom. And across the stream and up a canyon on our neighbors' property was Coyote Canyon, home to many generations of coyotes.

The deeply wooded, fern-covered cliffs that Laird had dubbed

"The Grotto of Our Lady of Perpetual Tears" dried up in the drought of 1988. He regretfully changed the name to "The Grotto of Our Lady of Intermittent Tears."

The main field, known prosaically as the Marshall Field, was guarded by a stately open-grown bur oak with widespread limbs, inevitably named the Grand Marshall Oak. To track burnings, we divided the fields into Marshall Fields One, Two, and Three (and sometimes Four, depending on how ambitious a burn we decided to do and how we divided up the burn units).

Beyond the Marshall Fields, beyond the bend in the path, the high-rolling hillsides that faced the marsh and pine relict are known as the Daisy Meadows—once again, One, Two, and Three. Daisy Meadow One had lupine, blackberries, and abundant prairie plants: liatris, little bluestem, and coreopsis, to name a few—that spread with each successful burn. The oak forest crept down from above, its acorns sprouting into scrawny settlers.

Daisy Meadow Two was very sandy and had bright gold puccoons in the spring, if the wild turkeys didn't scratch them up; also blue-eyed grass, Indian hemp, and milkweed. Daisy Meadow Three had fewer interesting plants but was higher and had a splendid view overlooking an old willow marsh. We dreamed of putting a tent platform here or a bench for bird-watching. In the woods above the third Daisy Meadow, the purple-flowered shooting stars were thickest in May. One spring I relocated some to a new home behind the cabin, where they thrived.

At the end of the third Daisy Meadow, where our land met the DNR land beyond, was the Last Apple Tree. Once again, the name served as a guidepost. I could observe, for instance, "There are more shooting stars by the Last Apple Tree this year," or, "The blackberries are growing in too thickly by the Last Apple Tree."

I treasured the apples off this little ancient tree for a couple of years and strove mightily to rejuvenate it. I climbed it in March to prune the tangled branches and hung containers of sweet solution to entice and drown the codling moths. But I wouldn't spray

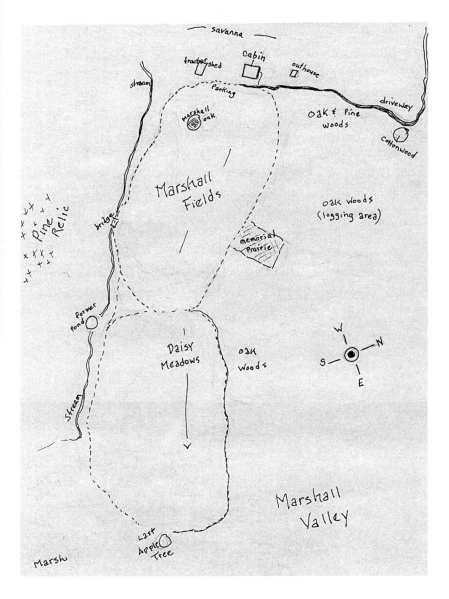

poisons, and the apples, though bursting with flavor, remained small, warty, and mildewy. They also hosted a few worms, and gathering and slicing enough apples to create a sensational pie became more effort than I was willing to put in. Each year the apples diminished, making me very sad because the flavor of these apples—vividly tart on your tongue—far surpassed that of the shiny red globes in the supermarket. I daydreamed of cloning that tree, another in the vast catalogue of unrealized valley daydreams.

A stream ran along the southwest edge of the Marshall Fields, vigorous and babbling, its banks heavily overgrown with jewel weed in summer. It was too shallow for trout, though the fishermen amongst our friends kept hoping. We never dignified it with a name; it was always the stream, home of an occasional beaver, destined for the watershed and ultimately the Wisconsin River.

Wild sunflower and angelica on the stream banks towered above our heads. One makeshift bridge that kept washing away let us cross, precariously. Across the stream the path up to the pine relict, shadowy and spongy among the thick stand of young pines, was known as Turkey Run because of the frequent splatters of wild turkey droppings. Occasionally we would disturb a turkey, who would take off for a safe roost with an exasperated flurry of ruffled wings. At the end of Turkey Run, where the path led upward through rocks and tree roots, ever steeper, was the prime treasure: the pine relict, a high rocky outcropping where giant pines hovered over a typical northern understory. We dubbed it Piney Point.

I drew maps over the years to identify where the various features were located. But mapmaking, it turns out, was not one of my abilities, especially with such oddly shaped property. Ultimately we found a young man with better cartography skills who created a scale map that allowed us to identify both the gradation and major land uses.

Gradually, as we came to know and describe the lay of the land, our plans for it, likewise, took shape.

Confronting the Challenge

A thing is right when it tends to preserve the integrity,
stability and beauty of the biotic community.
> —ALDO LEOPOLD, *A SAND COUNTY ALMANAC*

Good Guys and Bad Guys

I've observed that to a four-year-old, ethical imperatives are very simple. There are good guys and bad guys, and we should protect and care for the good guys and help to subdue the bad guys. When I gave my grandson Sam a bird book and bird feeder, it didn't take him long to identify who was who. The owls were bad because they picked on the other birds. The cowbirds were bad because they were lazy. They didn't build their own nests, instead laying eggs in other birds' nests, where their rowdy young would push the smaller, weaker birds aside. Hawks, of course, were bad. Soon he moved on from birds to other life-forms. Meat-eating dinosaurs were bad, and plant-eating dinosaurs were good. He had a little trouble with squirrels, who insisted on attacking the bird feeder. Until then, they had been acceptable.

Plants are more difficult for a four-year-old to categorize, since they all look more or less alike. I introduced him to garlic mustard as I tried to rid his yard of it in Cincinnati, but plants didn't hold his attention the way birds, and certainly dinosaurs, did.

Still, I envied him his ability to classify with such certainty. Adults are so hampered by nuance that they struggle to make choices.

Take, for instance, honeysuckle. When everyone told us we had to get rid of it, Laird balked. "It's so pretty—why should we?" So we were lackadaisical in our approach while this monstrous botanical tyrant (an invasive Asian cousin of the domestic brand) ran wild along our paths and up into the woodlands, shading out everything in a six-foot radius and spreading like chickenpox.

What to encourage, and what to eliminate? I got the *Wisconsin Manual of Control Recommendations for Ecologically Invasive Plants,* put out by the DNR Bureau of Endangered Resources. Lest anyone think ecologically invasive plants are a minor nuisance, the reality is much more serious. Ecologists now classify invasive plants as the second largest threat to native plants and wildlife, after only habitat destruction and way ahead of pollution. An ecologist friend of mine said he would put them first, since it's possible to do something about habitat destruction and almost impossible to control invasive species, at least on a large scale.

Of the top nineteen most threatening invasives, I identified six that were already established at the valley and on their way to becoming nuisances. And of those, honeysuckle, reed canary grass, multiflora rose, and wild parsnip topped my list. Each was aggressive, outcompeted natives, and was hard to control. Real bad guys, as my grandson would put it. And like any underdog preparing to fight the bad guys, we needed a plan.

Readying for Battle

One of the first things we bought was a secondhand tractor. David found one, and as a mechanical engineer, he was the one who kept it running. Mowing paths around the perimeter of the valley helped with prairie burns and allowed access to stream banks and made for a good walking path. Laird named the tractor Gerald, after our thirty-eighth president. "It's a Ford," he said. "It isn't flashy, but it gets the job done."

In the first week of June, Laird was mowing paths, and I was dressed in my high rubber boots, jeans, and long-sleeved denim shirt, wearing goggles and a hat. With a four-gallon tank of Roundup strapped to my back (before it was discovered to be hazardous to health) I waded up the stream. It was a hot day, but the coolness of the water and the birds along the stream bank kept me more or less content. I was spraying swaths of reed canary grass, which I had been able to keep barely in check with this yearly spraying. Sometimes I stepped on a deep muddy part of the stream bottom and sank into muck deeper than my boots. My feet getting progressively squishier, I clambered over trees and branches that had fallen down across the stream. With the heavy tank on my back, this was strenuous labor.

A tufted titmouse called, "Peter—peter—peter," in his insistent crescendo. It was a particularly lovely day, but there were other things I would rather be doing.

Ironically, well-meaning land managers for years had been planting reed canary grass, a Eurasian variant of a native grass, to control stream bank erosion. Even Laird's father had apparently planted it around his new fishpond, from where it spread along the stream, choking out everything in its path and creating a thick impermeable mat of vegetation that was unattractive to birds, animals, and people. Where stream banks used to be covered with native angelica, tall meadow rue, jewel weed, marsh marigolds—all attended with devotion by hummingbirds, swallows, and various dragonflies—now only a dense growth of reed canary grass, deserted by wildlife, remained.

Biologists had been researching this pest, but so far, I learned, had found no effective means of control. Suggested treatments included spraying with herbicide when the seed heads begin to form in late May and early June and regular mowing (nearly impossible in our situation because of the terrain).

And so, each June, I sprayed. Sometimes I could corral Laird into sharing this task with me, but frequently he found other essential duties to occupy him. After all, he was the one who kept things running when David was not around—like the tractor and generator.

At least we had more options for controlling the honeysuckle. When small, it can be pulled out. When larger, it must be cut off at ground level and painted with herbicide. David also designed a wickedly clever device, which he named a "honeysickle," that pries the younger honeysuckle right out of the ground, thus obviating the clipping and painting procedure. The only problem was that the honeysuckle had spread so far that there was barely a corner of these 115 acres without a cluster of its bright leaves, waving cheerily, blooming sweetly in May and bursting forth with red berries in the fall. The birds were delighted with the berries. They ingested them and excreted them everywhere, planting yet more new sprouts. The honeysuckle was ubiquitous.

If I cut twenty honeysuckle a day for the next ten years, would I make a dent? Perhaps. Of course, that assumes year-round diligence. One summer I spent many hard-labor hours cutting honeysuckle along the creek and driveway, and when one of my friends came out, she casually mentioned, "I see you're letting your honeysuckle grow."

That year for my birthday, Laird gave me a battery-powered Sawzall, a wonderful implement for those with chain-saw fear. A hand tool, it can be fitted out with different blades to cut just about anything—and one blade is perfect for honeysuckle. My crusade became a little easier.

Wild parsnip found its own way to torment us. This bushy green plant, vigorous and intrusive, of course, has a wicked toxin in the leaves and stem that causes a nasty rash on your skin if you rub against it on a sunny day and forget to wash immediately. At its worst, the rash will blister and leave purple scars for months afterward. I grieved when both of my grandchildren got blisters on their cheeks when they were too short to keep their exposed skin above the toxic leaves.

Wild parsnip likes to grow anywhere the soil has been disturbed. It was particularly happy on the path we mowed around the circumference of the fields. In June it develops a bright yellow flower similar to Queen Anne's lace, to which it is related. Within six days, it goes to seed and plants future colonies that will spread and crowd out anything in the vicinity. One year the path along the stream was almost solid with wild parsnip, with other paths noticeably afflicted. I realized that the deer hunters, trying to be helpful, had cut it when it had gone to seed, and it spread vigorously.

Mowing the parsnip between the time of flowering and seeding can greatly discourage its growth. Unfortunately, since Gerald, the tractor, was often broken—and most assuredly was broken at any critical time—we had let the parsnip go to seed too many times. Another deterrent would have been to spray each individual with Roundup, which I knew to be a leviathan task, or to dig up each individually, equally overwhelming.

I decided once to see whether wild parsnip could be eaten, since I do dearly love domestic parsnips. Handling them carefully, with gloves, I dug up a few and fixed them much the same way, sautéed in butter, with added parsley. Sure enough, they tasted the same. I told Laird that if all else failed, we could live out here and exist on blackberries, apples, and wild parsnip!

We did make a concerted effort one summer and pulled out a whole truckload of parsnip, using a clever narrow spade-like implement called a Parsnip Predator, a modified shovel that quickly cuts the roots and stem at the required depth. Since then it's been fairly easy to spot and destroy the remaining intruders.

As we attempted to rid ourselves of these pests, we kept discovering new ones. Every one of my botanist-type friends who visited found something—autumn olive, sweet clover, Canada thistle, multiflora rose—that had to be removed "immediately." Sometimes I felt like Job with his battery of trials.

Meanwhile, a consensus was growing among some nature lovers that battling invasives is a losing—and perhaps even damaging—effort. The long-term effects of Roundup and other herbicides needed to be thoroughly analyzed. Evidence was mounting that its widespread use encourages the growth of Roundup-resistant weeds. This was particularly noticeable in farm fields. I started using it more judiciously than I had at first, learning every day that bad guys and good guys could not easily be categorized.

Of course, many experts were eager to offer advice. Bob Read, although a DNR wetlands ecologist, wanted us to let the whole valley grow up in pines. Hugh Iltis, botanist and director of the herbarium at the University of Wisconsin–Madison, suggested we light a match at one end of the valley and let it all burn. Someone else—a prairie lover—wanted us to remove all the pines from the bottomland and concentrate on the prairie. We found an early DNR file that described the pine relict in great scientific detail. The writer urged the DNR to purchase the land if possible—and to keep invasives out. It seems that the specialists could tell us what to get rid of but couldn't tell us how!

Honeybees and Bluebirds

David and Shelley were interested in raising bees and harvesting honey, so within the first year or so they brought several hives and a population of bees and settled them in by the old fallen-down barn. They read and researched and came with real beekeeping equipment—white suits and hats with mesh masks. For a few years they did reasonably well, collecting quarts of excellent honey, but one tragedy after another seemed to beset the hives: The bees developed a disease called Nosema. Queens deserted. Hives collapsed. The project either had to be abandoned or moved to safer surroundings. They moved the hives elsewhere.

Another project was the establishment of a bluebird trail. After attending a meeting of the local bluebird society about how to care for the houses and ensure safe fledging of offspring, we put up about five bluebird houses, surrounded with baffles to keep out the snakes and raccoons. We saw bluebirds around, and when we checked the houses there was evidence of nest making—often interlayered with nests of wrens or swallows.

It was unfortunate that we didn't live there and tend them regularly. In most of the houses, wrens or swallows triumphed. We might have raised one family of bluebirds, but often our houses were sites of tragedies. Snakeskins were evidence of marauders; broken eggs beneath the nest suggested another kind of marauder, perhaps raccoons, who had been troublesome in the past. On one

beautiful May evening, I had
written of their escapades,

> We reposition the bird
> feeder to thwart the
> raccoons—putting it
> further out on the branch.
> But in the night, I hear them,
> and sit up. Two big furry critters
> with gold headlights—one has climbed right up the
> anchor rope to the feeder and is tipping seed down to
> the one below! I wake Laird and he yells at them in "raccoon
> speak." I have a feeling they will always outsmart us.

We bought PVC piping and encased the posts to prevent critters from crawling up. Over the years we did our best to maintain the nests and pull out the unwanted invaders, but this project too was doomed. The houses aged and fell over and were gradually removed.

Laird and I took on a more promising project: to resuscitate the orchard that had once been planted here by an earlier owner. At least a dozen apple trees were scattered along the hillsides, and as each variety ripened we sampled the fruit for taste and consistency. There were early sweet red apples and larger green apples that ripened later. The best ones ripened in the fall. Some were yellow and crisp and sweet, and we managed to get a few pies out of them. To remember which tree had which kind of apple so that we'd know where to put our attention to pruning and tending, we made labels describing taste, texture, and season. The labels were on three-by-five-inch cards inside plastic bags, attached to the trees with twist ties.

We felt very smug about our scheme and were eager to check on our trees the following spring. Lo and behold, the deer had nibbled off every plastic bag—why, and whether they were trying to digest them, we couldn't imagine.

It was becoming obvious that this was not to be a working, moneymaking farm, if that's what we had wanted it to be. To make it so would have taken more diligent and constant care. Our admiration for farmers grew. We turned our attention to restoration of the woods and prairies and gave up on food production. The one crop that we managed to harvest was berries: black raspberries in early summer, and blackberries at summer's end. And we still knew the two best apple trees for pie making and managed to be there sometimes at the right season.

We did succeed in keeping hummingbirds happy with the feeder we hung on the deck, keeping it filled with hummingbird nectar and enjoying these beautiful if fractious little visitors for many years.

Easing into Green

My journal for Saturday, June 17, 1989, describes the natural splendor of early summer that greeted us that wonderful shiny afternoon:

> Daisies have burst out in the past week. Catbird sits in the catbird seat and chortles incessantly. We cut cherry and box elder in the prairie, and a few sumac. After supper we walk to the third daisy meadow and put up folding chairs to watch the birds in the marsh, but we're late and they're all tucked in for the night. Nice pink sunset and incredible moon! Go into Ridgeway for ice cream.

By late summer, the field was a mosaic of greens in subtle shades—yellow-green, emerald-green, with here and there a yellow spire of gray-headed coneflower, its gray-brown head asserting itself, high and thimble shaped. The yellow petals, curving downward, reminded me of ballet dancers' skirts swirling mid-pirouette, so much that I expected to see tiny ballet slippers poking out. At the end of August in our fourth year of prairie visits, the goldenrod seemed ready to burst. One or two little flowerettes on tall heads had opened early, like heralds announcing that next week gold will own the field.

Dogwood clones stood out as purple-brown mounds, like

islands in a green lake. We had burned the field to keep the trees from coming in, but it didn't deter the dogwood, and a few wild cherries also persisted, thrusting their plumes skyward. And of course the grand bur oak that laughed at fires stood rangy and ruffled, still densely green: a dominant presence. The oak had guarded the valley for several centuries. It shaded the farmer who tried to scratch out a living in this isolated spot over a hundred years ago. Maybe it was there when the Ho-Chunk camped by the stream, as they surely must have done.

When we would tramp through the field on our quest for blackberries, we stirred up dozens of springing crickets and other insects I couldn't name. They fell silent as we approached and resumed the concert as we passed. In late summer, their high whine was as much a part of the afternoon as the heavy air, the intensity of green, the gray weathered wood of deck and picnic table, the steep hillsides, mottled sky, and faint roar of trucks on Highway 151.

There must have been many kinds of insects at work or at play. If I listened closely to the din, sorting out the various layers, I detected a constant shrillness, pulsed by secondary beats to create a syncopated rhythm. An insect symphony. In the tall trees a few crows squawked, but the birdsongs had dwindled dramatically from earlier in the summer: no persistent, harrying wren, no towhee. The bluebird couple had fled—to where I couldn't imagine, but I hoped the young ones they had been feeding so diligently in July survived predators to fledge and accompany their parents.

As the afternoon shaded into dusk, the hum of insects dropped by about an octave. I like to think the little shrill ones were put to bed and now the adults sang on, but I suppose there's a better entomological explanation. Whatever the reason, their evening and night chorus was a softer, more soothing, chirrupy sound.

Wrapped in my well-loved habitat, I reveled in the peace that always enveloped me there and awaited the warm rush, like the glow from a good martini. But I found it missing that day. Instead of melting into the surroundings like another lump of organic material, I was the stranger, the invader: uneasy, apprehensive. I could feel the symptoms of responsibility.

At times the thought of all the care the place needed overwhelmed me: the reed canary grass, the gray dogwood that turned the open woodland along the path into an impenetrable thicket. The poplars and willows we had mowed on the prairie were returning, more vigorous than ever. Constantly fighting these persistent invaders led to a strong feeling of being at war with nature rather than being at one with it. I needed to remind myself that the valley was not really ours; we were only visitors. We had to do what we could to repair damage done by miners and farmers, but in the long run nature was our landlord, and we were only renters.

In the dimming light of that overcast day, that magical shaft of sunlight appeared from the ridge behind my right shoulder. Like melted butter, it streamed across the field and up into the treetops, for a long moment of benediction. Then it darkened to shadow.

We ate dinner on the deck and read inside as long as our eyes could hold out in the dimness of the gas lights. Laird drowsed with his head in my lap, his book sliding off his chest. Then we pulled on sleeping clothes—sufficient to beat the chill—turned off the kerosene lights, and crawled under blankets on the mattresses we dragged onto the deck. A gentle pattering of raindrops alighted on the roof. Beyond the far hills we could see a glow from the baseball diamond in Ridgeway and the intrusive speck of red light on top of the town water tower. Otherwise, only the intermittent pinpoint of a late-season firefly hyphenated the soft gray night. I heard the flutter of our friendly bats taking off from their home under the eaves, clearing away mosquitoes.

When I woke around five, the sky had cleared, and the remains of a lopsided moon hung over Lookout Point next to Orion, which was sprawled above the tree line. Moonlight infused the mist with gauzy light. If this were May there'd be a wild cacophony of bird notes, but now there were none. I missed those noisy little wrens and the turkeys gobbling. Suddenly, a tiny scream from the woods broke the stillness as some poor rabbit met his owl-doom. Then silence again, and I dozed off.

Not as Much Fun

In 1997 our stalwart companions, David and Shelley, moved north to their own prairie and bog acreage in central Wisconsin, to our lasting regret. We missed their knowledge, guidance, and inspiration, as well as their labor!

We continued with our various projects, following tips from experts and information gleaned at workshops. On this day, I had set myself to eradicate the bramble on the dry prairie, which we called the Memorial Prairie in honor of Laird's parents. When we first took notice, this sandy half-acre slope was closing in with sumac, but I could see the prairie plants underneath, crying out for sunshine. So we cut and burned the sumac, and the lovely hillside is thriving now, a prairie vision in little and big bluestem, prairie liatris, tall bush clover, spiderwort, coreopsis, baptisia, harebells, downy gentians, and many more. But halfway up, a snarly growth of bramble was spreading: dewberry, a creeping cousin of blackberry. We tried pulling it up. We burned it many times. Nothing fazed it. It came up healthier and more vigorous than before and spread its canopy of leaves. One year I carefully sprayed the leaves with Roundup, but it dripped off and annihilated a big patch of bluestem.

Someone told us that we could wear cotton gloves over rubber gloves, dip our hands in Roundup and run them up the stem and leaves. I tried it, of course, and found it to be a messy and totally unsatisfactory process, especially when the rubber gloves leaked and I could feel the poison squishing inside.

I considered leaving the bramble alone. It was a native species, after all. But if it was shading more desirable plants, I thought I should try to remove it. So that year, I scrooched myself around the hillside on my bottom, cutting each tiny bramble stem and then, before the toothpick-sized stump got lost in the grasses, painted it with Brush-be-Gone with a tiny paintbrush.

Unfortunately I had waited until July, when I should have tried this earlier in the summer when it was at peak vigorous growth. But there were other things. As I worked, as the sun beat down and fried my ears where I forgot to rub sunscreen, I knew it might not work and might have to be repeated. The valley hummed, buzzed, and pulsed with life and living: the cacophony of billions of microscopic cells, all singing hallelujah. Puffy clouds like dollops of whipped cream floated in a blue ocean of sky. Song sparrows chirped and trilled. Nearby a catbird shrieked imprecations at me. I had invaded her space.

I slid upwards and confronted yet another clump: one, two, three, four, five snips. Next I painted them. The fumes were making my nose run. Alas, I supposed they were quite toxic, and once again I was attacking my body along with the weeds. Was I crazy? As I pondered the question, all around me, the valley sang out its cryptic answer.

Days of Wonder

*When despair for the world grows in me . . . I come into
the peace of wild things who do not tax their lives with
forethought of grief.*
    —WENDELL BERRY, "THE PEACE OF WILD THINGS"

Sharing the Splendor

Once we had the cabin at least minimally civilized, we couldn't wait to introduce people to our wonderful valley. The journal I kept noted visitors and picnics practically every weekend. We enjoyed sharing the land with friends and neighbors, coworkers, relatives—anyone who showed an interest.

Most first-time visitors had to exclaim about the driveway. We were used to it, but for people expecting paved or even gravel roads, it was a challenge. Not much more than a steep path, it wound around several sharp curves, over a culvert, and finally down on the flat stretch toward the cabin. After a storm, branches of formidable size might add an additional layer of treachery—although we knew to bring along a chain saw to clear them in order to get ourselves through. Depending on how much rain had fallen, the small stream that ran alongside might have left puddles or small lakes in the driveway.

"Do you call that a driveway?" "Is it a goat path?" "We thought we were lost!" and various other remarks were common. Some dear friends drove down in an ancient VW bug, and the battery dropped out through the rotting floorboards!

We would always shrug and say, "It keeps the riff-raff out." It would have been very expensive to straighten and improve it, losing trees in the process, and to be quite honest, we liked it the way it was.

Part of every invitation usually included a stroll around the
Marshall Fields, and on around the bend in the path below the
daisy meadows and oak woods. In spring we walked to the top of
the first daisy meadow to check out the lupine and bird's-foot vio-
lets, and on to the second meadow where the puccoon bloomed
so reliably. At the top of the third daisy meadow, we pointed
out shooting stars in the woods and a view down across a wet
meadow where there was always good bird-sighting. Depending
on the vigor of the guests, we might cross the stream (if the latest
bridge hadn't floated away), wind our way through deep woods
to the base of the pine relict, and coax them to clamber up and
look over the edge in awe. Back at the cabin we'd refresh ourselves
with beer and food, either via potluck or a cookout over the fire
pit in front of the cabin.

In October of 1988, we invited family, friends, and fellow conservation enthusiasts out to the valley for a special event that we
called the Marshall Memorial Meander, in celebration of Laird's
parents and the land they had gifted to us. That year the Nature
Conservancy honored us by dedicating the land as Marshall Valley and gave us a plaque recognizing our efforts at restoration. I
described our delight at being able to share the valley that day in a
journal entry:

> A splendid occasion. Fan Taylor
> presents a plaque from the Nature
> Conservancy, honoring our
> efforts to tend the valley!
> We're very honored, and
> it will hang on the cabin wall
> for as long as we are the
> caretakers! . . . Sunny and
> warm, colors just beginning.
> We take a walk to see where the gen-
> tians are just blooming on the dry prairie.

gentian

The Lady Beetles Hatch

Then there was the day the Asian lady beetles hatched and nearly drove me crazy. It was October and unusually warm, hazy, and sunny. I came out alone on a Friday to meet a contractor. Laird and I had started to talk about upgrading the cabin. The foundations were cracking and buckling; the siding had been eaten away in back by carpenter ants—and of course we were always tempted by the idea of running water. After we talked for a while, the contractor assured me that no self-respecting contractor or subcontractor would tackle a job there if he had to negotiate "that godawful driveway." He gave me the name of his brother, who was a road builder, and then he left.

I was blissfully alone. The sun on the deck was hot, and as I sat at the picnic table, making lists of things to do, I started to notice everywhere around me a moving traffic of little orange lady beetles. In perpetual motion, they crawled up the posts, along the beams and railing. They were everywhere, filling the air with their pinging and springing flights. They landed on my nose and my glasses and invaded my ears. They landed upside down in my glass of water and waved their legs furiously. They stank if crushed.

I tried to be patient and benevolent. They were supposed to be harmless—or even helpful. Imported from China by well-meaning soybean farmers specifically to rid crops of aphids, they had no natural predators and so multiplied and wandered far afield. I couldn't even sit and read without having six or eight crawl on me, scuttling up and down the pages. Finally, I snapped. I went for the Raid can, which we used to fight the carpenter ants. The pine posts that supported the deck roof were the beetles' major thoroughfares. They looked like the Los Angeles thruway at rush hour, jammed only with VWs. Some were a bright red, some tan, some gold. Some of them had lots of spots, and others had none at all.

The Raid didn't slow them down. They continued to land annoyingly on my face and chin, any handy promontory, and it was driving me buggy. Frustrated, I went for a walk. A few were in the fields and woods, but clearly their main staging area was the deck as they staked out shelter for the winter. This was one time the wilderness was more hospitable for humans than the house.

That was the first year of the winged invaders. In years after, they continued to return, although never again in such a mass. Some of them wintered over in the walls of the cabin and crawled out sleepily in spring. We learned to expect them, to know their habits, and to sweep them out the door in spring, along with the dead flies.

Blackberry Musings

It was August, blackberry season. Laird had bought a box at the farmer's market the previous week, but they were so tasteless that most of them ended up in the compost pile. We were eager to try out our own crop. Attired in boots, long sleeves, and bug spray, we headed for the middle of the field, where they ripened first. Wading through springy grasses, massed cinquefoil, and tall bush clover, we caught a whiff of mint from crushed monarda, or bee balm, still holding its last ragged petals.

When the brambles started to snag our ankles we knew we were in blackberry territory, and sure enough I saw their spiny stalks bent to the weight of multicolored berries—pale pink, bright red, darker red, and the heavy black ripe "king berries." We picked only the finest—thumbnail-sized, with each rounded seed pouch fat and full of flavor.

The previous spring, we had a good hot burn in this field, and Laird mowed paths through and around the patches. All of that made the picking much easier, removing the tall brutal dead stalks—the picker's torment. The bushes were shorter because they didn't have as much competition. Some of the fattest berries were at knee level. Laird insisted that each stalk required a taste test. I said one berry per clump was enough. But he argued, "I had two plants side by side, and on one the berries were sweet enough to make you cry, and the other had no taste at all." So we taste tested—and he was right, as usual. All blackberries are not created equal. Some that look like pictures from the seed catalogue are disappointingly bland, while little runty nubbins might burst with flavor.

As we browsed the field, we were on the lookout for the grassy nests hidden among the bushes where perhaps a fawn had slept last night, and might be yet, having been taught to stay perfectly still. One spring we nearly stepped on a spotted baby about as big as a Labrador retriever pup. Its ears were alert, only its brown eyes in motion, liquid and wary. By now, that baby would be fully grown and hiding in the woods, perhaps with her own fawn.

As our buckets filled, we noticed that something small had been eating bites of the berries and spitting the seeds out on the leaves below. A tiny worm cemented itself to the berry and to a leaf, so that it was sandwiched between—assuring protection and provisions for offspring, I suppose. Our berry patches were entire ecosystems, sustaining vast populations of happy feeders. We amused ourselves by pretending to be hunter-gatherers, living off the land. We picked till we had more than we needed but still couldn't stop. "Just one more—here's one that's too good." That night I would dream of blackberries—tart, tongue-tantalizing mounds of blackberries.

Blackberry season would go on for several weeks. The next weekend, I went off to pick some more berries while Laird wrote lesson plans on the deck for his math class. We made short work of the first batch on cereal and ice cream. Ending up with far more than we could use, we were able to be generous to our neighbors back in town and to the scavengers who would come after we left. They grow in profusion in this valley, many more than we could wish, and most of the year we cursed them fervently for invading our favorite meadow and crowding out the spring lupine. The bushes reached lethal arms across paths, grabbing collars, snatching off caps, coiling viciously around ankles.

Blackberries are one of the most vigorous members of the bramble, or *Rubus*, family, which means they are related to roses. According to *A Field Guide to Trees and Shrubs*, the Peterson guide by George Petrides, "Most bramble is a woody, prickly, or bristly shrub that causes problems to the specialist." The guide was referring to problems of identification. We knew about the other problems.

Nevertheless, in late August, when the berries started to ripen, we called a temporary truce in our battle, plunged shoulder deep into their hostile ranks, and plucked the largesse.

This was a fantastic berry year—enough rain to fatten them and enough sun to give them flavor. Since I had picked in the middle of the field last time, I headed through the woods to the top of the daisy meadow where, at the juncture of the oak woods and open hillside, a huge snarly patch thrived. The bushes that had entered the edge of the woods grew unusually tall and hugged the tree limbs, so that I had to reach over my head to pick the berries.

Mora is the Italian word for blackberry. I know because it was my favorite flavor of gelato when I lived in Rome: cold, seductively tart. Sighing in remembrance, I plucked another handful. These berries were larger than the ones down in the field—sometimes over an inch long, and the branches were more heavily weighted than I could ever remember. I counted nearly forty berries from one stalk alone—and that didn't include the overripe few that dropped to the ground or the still unripened red ones that I would retrieve the next week.

I liberated only the ones that gave up easily. If they were still holding on tight, I didn't want them. I could fill my bucket in a patch about six feet square, but I liked to roam and didn't quit till they were rolling off the top of the bucket, my hands torn and bleeding, the gnats and mosquitoes having penetrated my layer of bug spray and stickers having worked their way into my socks.

It was a hot afternoon, and sweat trickled down inside my shirt. Blackberry picking was not for the faint-hearted.

These berries would be baked in a cobbler—layered in a baking dish with a cup or so of sugar, covered with a shortcake crust, baked for fifteen or twenty minutes and served hot with real cream. We would eat it for breakfast and again for supper (maybe with ice cream) and never get tired of it.

Some might go in an apple pie to enhance the color and taste. Any berries that didn't go in our stomachs right away or to neighbors would be frozen whole in plastic containers. Next winter we would cook them with a little sugar and kirsch or triple sec and serve them over ice cream, thinking of our bounteous beautiful valley.

Gathering Seed

A stillness hangs over the valley in late September—a waiting, breathless stillness. The chirruping, chortling songbirds are gone, as are the tiny aggressive hummers. The field is still mostly green, but patchy with brown, plum, and fiery red sumac. On the hillsides, a few birches and poplars are yellowing, first defectors in the wall of green. Lone birds give plaintive, one-note cries. Jays wheedle. Only the chickadees seem jolly and playful. In little social groups they flit from willow to willow, whistling their sassy "dee-dee-dee."

On a warm, T-shirt afternoon, I gathered seeds. Many were ripe by early fall, and sliding or nipping them off their stems was a strangely sensuous occupation. Maybe it stirred some primordial sense of harvest, laying in stores. But these seeds were not for sustenance in the long winter, but rather to plant a new/old plot of prairie, in my unending labor to restore what once was here.

The field, still dotted by native plants, was a prairie once— or perhaps an oak savanna. Perhaps whoever farmed the land around the turn of the twentieth century had burned it to keep it from growing up in poplar, willow, and dogwood, the same way we did. By the time the land came into our possession, vigorous goldenrod, bramble, and non-native grasses were dominant. Some varieties of goldenrod are wonderful—the stiff goldenrod, showy goldenrod, and the wonderful zigzag goldenrod that grows on the savanna. Unfortunately the field had been over-run with aggressive Canada goldenrod that resents any attempt at integration. It elbows out every other species and creates a near-monoculture. Some other plants survived. That day I admired the asters—white, blue, and purple—that had forced their way in happy profusion among the browning stalks of goldenrod. And I planned to help them—the asters and other less vigorous natives who were just looking for their chance to compete. I tried a little affirmative action.

The plan was to spray Roundup on a patch about twenty by twenty feet dominated by goldenrod, cinquefoil, bramble, and the like. When it had been cleared of competitors and the Roundup had dissipated, I would seed it in with the mixture of grasses and forbs (flowering plants) I had collected from other areas. Then next year another patch or two, and more each year, and as they spread, the prairie would reassert itself. Maybe before I died I would have a chance to see it as it once was. This was the plan.

There had been many plans, and many experts and many books—as well as many failures. And all of that served to make me very humble.

I found a patch of Indian grass, the most obliging, waving its heavy-headed graceful plumes, and started my collection. The ripened seeds slipped off easily. As I pinched the stalk and slid my fingers upward, they filled my palm, a handful of silken kernels. I took perhaps a third or less of the seeds, leaving the rest to drop and increase the size of this patch. Bee balm and mountain mint both exhaled a wonderful scent as I plucked their crisp heads, and the round-headed bush clover sported fuzzy brown tassels.

The big bluestem fought me more—perhaps not quite ready. Some of the seed clumps were way above my head. Big bluestem is what the westward settlers saw in mile upon mile of rolling distance—big bluestem, with stems and leaves a rosy tan, ripened seed heads splayed like turkey feet.

Up on the prairie, the much shorter little bluestem had burst its seeds into delicate stars that slid off easily in my hand when I ran it up the tawny stems. My paper sack filled. I climbed to the top of this hill and rested on the bench we built years ago, chewed by woodchucks now on all its corners. We called this the Marshall Memorial Prairie because the ashes of Laird's parents rest here. A journal entry from April 29, 1989, notes, "This day, Jan and Owen and Meg and Laird and Alice did lay John and Sally at rest at the top of the Marshall Memorial Prairie." It was their valley, and they loved it. We plan to join them here one day.

From the bench I could look down across this narrow hillside of vigorous dry prairie and, at least here, see the success of all my labors. It was a tangled mass of sumac and bramble when I first saw it, and over the years, with a lot of burning and sweaty labor, it had regained its birthright—thick clumps of little bluestem bend rosy stalks, shimmering in the September sun. Here beside the bench, I could see downy gentians poking inky-blue faces from among the grasses and wondered, why did I ever leave? This place was my feast, my art gallery, my symphony. My eyes blurred. Everything else seemed far away.

Engineers of the Prairie

Carpenters, despoilers, and the farmer's scourge, beavers are nature's army corps of engineers. In our first years at the valley, we had a number of different beaver ponds—each year, a new surprise—one year by the Marshall oak, one year at the bend in the stream beyond the tractor shed. The beavers always found a ready supply of small tender poplars, which we would just as soon have removed. And the beavers were endlessly industrious, weaving their pointy sticks into impenetrable walls, thickly cemented with mud.

Behind the dam, a murky pond would build, eventually flooding whatever was growing around it. They carefully left a little spillway for the stream to trickle through, so that it would not be completely impounded. Sometimes the water would rise up over the stream banks, but the resulting ponds never grew large enough to concern us. After all, we were not growing crops, and the native plants had their own ways of adapting. The pond surfaces were scummed over and busy with floating bugs, twigs, and leaves: beaver heaven.

As I learned more about beavers, my admiration continued to grow for the clever rascals. Domestic and family centered, they tended their pups with watchful care. Observing and anticipating them each spring was one of our biggest pleasures.

One year a whole series of temporary or experimental dams

appeared along the stretch of stream closest to the cabin, and we named them Aswan, Boulder, and Coulee. The following year, new dams appeared elsewhere. The beavers seemed not to be able to make up their minds on location. For a couple of years, they were far out in the valley, in the marsh to the right of the path below the daisy meadows. There they constructed their most extensive effort, an engineering marvel with a hutch along the bank and three large shallow ponds, barricaded with long dams. The dams were broad and sturdy enough to walk along, and it was always fun to see the beavers' works in progress, or to catch a rare glimpse of one swimming—just a brown nose and two humps, with the tail creating a wide wake—or to hear the slap of a tail on the water surface, their alarm signal.

Beavers are very shy and rarely show themselves in the daytime. Apparently they became nocturnal when early trappers hunted them almost to extinction. For really good beaver viewing, you have to position yourself along the stream bank at night. There, squatted in the damp and shrillness of frog song

one night, we waited patiently and were rewarded with steady gnawing and splashing sounds. We turned a dim flashlight toward the sound and saw the beaver in the water with a three-inch log, chewing it to the desired size and shape, undaunted by our light. A smaller beaver swam nearby. He suddenly dove underwater, probably at some parental warning.

Unfortunately, neighbors or trespassers took it upon themselves to rid our land of "varmints," the mindset in rural areas being what it is, and we found the body of one floating in the stream with what appeared to be bullet holes. The others disappeared. At the Ridgeway Fireman's Ball, a neighbor sidled up to me and said, "Bet you were glad to have someone clear out them beaver!" I suddenly had an inkling of whose husband might have done so. I told her as plainly as I could how I felt about it, how sad we were, and she looked back as though I were speaking a foreign language. "Well, they was wreckin' your place!" she pronounced. She couldn't understand that we didn't think so.

Another group of beavers showed up a couple of years later but didn't stay. Maybe it was too populated for their taste, though we were usually there only on weekends, so they had plenty of time to be alone with their projects. We were mightily disappointed when they abandoned us. I went so far as to call the Wisconsin Department of Natural Resources to see whether we could import some—whether they had a stock of beavers that no one else wanted. The voice on the phone paused when I explained what I wanted. I think this might have been his first request for a rent-a-beaver, and he was not at all sure that he wasn't getting a prank call. Anyhow, it turned out that the DNR did not keep a ready supply of beavers.

"Wait till we have a wet year," he told us. "When the Wisconsin River backs up into the smaller streams, that's when they'll start trekking inland."

During a particularly wet year, we checked the stream banks regularly in hopes of spotting some gnawed stumps, some floating branches, with no luck. But it was a busy year, with construction noise from the new cabin. We held out hope they would find their way back and stake a claim on a section of stream when things quieted down.

The Approach of Fall

Fall brought sadness, as we enjoyed what might be our last night at the valley for the year. A thin skin of glossy white on the path, on the twigs, signaled it was time, as did the frost on the pump handle, its wet metal so cold that pumping the kettle full for dish washing was excruciating. Afterward, my hands were too cold still to hold the pen well. On one shivery September morning, I wrote,

> Cold in the night! The dishwater froze! At 4 a.m. the stars were immense and a little corner of moon over Lookout Point lit up the whole valley. At 7 a.m. the hoar frost turned every leaf and grass blade into silver.

As the sun shot its first rays along the edge of the meadow, ice crystals glistened, the prairie turned to rose, and cold mist rose in gauzy curtains.

Lying on the deck at seven in the morning, we were looking at a sky of intense blue, with pink clouds like a school of salmon swimming toward Lookout Point. As the sun gained height and bestowed some warmth on my right ear, I knew the day would be fine. The colors were magnificent, with the burnished red and wine of the oak leaves dominant.

I thought about the space of my surroundings—framed in continually changing borders of hills and cliffs, anchored by the long meadow in front of the cabin, and roofed over with a wide, generous sky. And of course the space seemed to open and expand in the fall, as the leaves let go. The feeling you got looking out at the valley from our high deck was similar to the feeling of looking at a lake or ocean—the mesmerizing distance, the changing light. Those who visited the valley for the first time—or many times—always climbed the steps to the deck, turned to look out, breathed in quickly, and said, "Ah."

Because of the way we were situated—low, with hills rising all around—the early morning light and the late afternoon light reached the meadow through notches in the hills as long fingers of light, creating ever-changing patterns of fire and shadow. The sumac would blaze; then it would darken, and the branches of the big oak appeared gilded. The birch suddenly shone rosy white. We watched to see where the last glow of evening would settle, pooling its gold glory, just for a moment, before withdrawing into dusk.

Something about looking at all this lovely space awakened within me a sense of awe and wonder, of continual fascination— as close to a spiritual feeling as I am able to express.

When I married my first husband, we lived in a little two-room apartment on the fifth floor of an old brick building in New York City. The view out the back was a brick wall; the view to the side was a fire escape and a brick wall. From a narrow little window in the corner of the bedroom, you could see a slice of 69th Street, and that's where I would sit while the babies were napping or the dinner cooking.

I did truly love, and still love, New York City, its pulsing roaring vitality, variety, life. But that little apartment closed me in with a suffocation that nearly destroyed me. My salvation was to bundle up the two little boys in their stroller and hit the streets; we walked and walked. We walked along the East River for hours, breathing in the distance, the murky water, the sky. Or we walked over to Central Park and found peace in its urban wilderness. Perhaps I suffer from claustrophobia. But I knew a special buoyancy of mind and spirit at the valley—even when I think about being at the valley.

On an October day, there was no sound but the hushed breath of the wind in the tall pines, an intermittent rattle of leaves, a distant yammering of crows. I reveled in the peace, knowing how much I would miss being here over the winter, counting down until spring opened up the road and warmed the deck.

Paths for the Ghost

Your ghost will walk, you lover of trees.
—ROBERT BROWNING, "DE GUSTIBUS"

The Standing Folk

My love affair with trees goes back as far as I can remember. Is it the Celtic blood, the songs of my ancient Druid forebears? In the fifth grade, I recited Joyce Kilmer's "Trees" in front of the whole school for Arbor Day: "I think that I shall never see, a poem lovely as a tree." Even then, I believed the words of the poet, loving the trees more than poetry. I had already learned to clamber up the big sycamores near our house on Long Island and perched high up, straddling the broad branches, peeling off loose bark, and thinking whatever young girls think about.

Even before I could climb, my favorite place to play was under the sheltering branches of the spruces that ringed our house—on their soft, spongy carpet, inhaling the sweet fragrance. Hidden from a brother's teasing and a grandmother's misconceived notions of what little girls should be doing, I created my own imaginary world, shaded and wind-whispered.

In the eighth grade when we were choosing our vocations, I announced that I would be a writer or forester—preferably both. I assumed that all foresters loved trees. How could they not? I imagined myself living in a lookout tower deep in the woods, putting out forest fires and writing novels.

We all know the saga of the great American forest: how the first European settlers arrived on this continent and found what appeared to be an endless ocean of trees. How they drove Native inhabitants from their land. How with short-sighted profligacy they cleared and burned it for farms and logged it for profit, foregoing sustainable forestry practices for widespread clear-cutting.

In its natural condition, Wisconsin was heavily wooded, but by the late 1800s many of the tall white pine, oak, maple, and walnut trees from northern Wisconsin and Minnesota had been harvested for ship masts, houses, and furniture. Some sections were spared, including reservation land that the Menominee fought to protect. The Menominee attempted to practice logging in a sustainable way—clearing only mature or fallen trees and planting to replace them—while battling the federal government for control of their land. Nevertheless, they set an example for more sustainable forestry practices that continue to this day.

The state's forests have rebounded somewhat in the past century, now covering about 46 percent of the total land area, according to the Wisconsin DNR. But because of the mass deforestation of the nineteenth and early twentieth centuries, most trees seen today are less than 125 years old. The amazing thing about trees is that they never give up. Wherever there's a patch of dirt, a slice of sunlight, they will find a way to sprout, uncurl a leaf or two in the first year, and keep reaching higher. Acorns from the white oak fall to the ground with their root sprout already sticking out a white finger. If they can survive the voracious appetites of grubs and deer and the stockpiling by squirrels, they can begin their journey skyward almost immediately. Oaks need light to regenerate, but seedlings can withstand fire, cutting, and deer browsing, and they will sprout again the same year. Maples can grow in dense shade and in turn will produce even denser shade when mature, thus defeating competition.

Recent research by scientists and other naturalists has revealed how trees appear to communicate with each other. Through a network of mycelia, or fungus, underground, they apparently exchange carbon, nitrogen, and phosphorus, warn one another of threats, and offer chemical assistance to the deprived. I was thrilled to read of this discovery but not surprised, as it supports my personal belief in the extraordinary powers of the natural world.

On the north-facing slope of our valley is what foresters call a pine relict. I looked this up in John Curtis's *Vegetation of Wisconsin*, where he describes the stands of relict pines in southern Wisconsin. More common in northern Wisconsin, the pine relicts of the Driftless can be dated to at least twelve thousand years ago based on the fossil pollen record, wrote Curtis. When a naturalist studied twenty-two of the Driftless pine relicts in 1950, he found some commonalities: all were on sandstone rocks dating to the Cambrian or Ordovician age, all were on sites with a slope of at least 40 degrees, and the associated plant life—huckleberry, pipsissewa, shinleaf, wintergreen, and Canada mayflower—resembled that of northern pine forests. And while farther south than was common, they seemed to be thriving.

One of the early visitors from the DNR told us about the relict when we first visited the valley, and it was always a favorite destination for us—as well as for various foresters and many other interested guests who asked for permission to visit. The forty-degree slope was relatively easy for younger visitors to maneuver, using rocks and small trees to find handholds. As legs grew older, the steepness of the slope seemed to increase. For the last ten or fifteen feet, we were crawling through a soft layer of pine needles and tree roots, at last arriving at the flattened top of the high bluff. Above us the majestic trees whispered in the breeze, dropping needles to add to the carpet below. We inhaled the intoxicating odor of pine. Here in the cool shadows, I could smell the breath of the Northwoods and hear the gentle whisper of feathered branches. Standing in the presence of these giants, their filtered sunlight and shadow, made one feel insignificant, an experience similar to standing in the soft light of an ancient cathedral, reverent and awed. Often we sat on the spongy carpet of pine needles, leaning against a tree, and talked softly, or not at all. To think that this was now ours was thrilling—if somewhat intimidating. Of course we didn't really think of it as ours, but as a marvelous piece of Wisconsin that we had the obligation to protect.

Walking among the pines, and the typical understory of herbs and shrubs that Curtis described, we noted that the terrain continued to slope upward, but more gradually. Through openings in the pine branches, we could see the cabin, small and far below at the head of the valley. Looking down over the edges of the bluff, we saw a heart-stopping plunge on one side—layers and layers of striated red and buff sandstone straight down about fifty feet. On the other side, the bluff sloped gradually into the woods below, tangled and wild. It was possible to climb down that way, but many large boulders and snarly branches created an obstacle course. Eventually we found a slope that we could slide down, slippery with pine needles and piles of leaves. Or we clambered down the way we had come.

On several occasions we were contacted by University of Wisconsin forestry researchers who were interested in the succession and age of the trees, the mixture of red and white pine, and the health of the understory. We also heard from archaeologists who thought Native rock art might be found somewhere under the lichen-encrusted rock faces and shallow caves, but, as far as we know, they have not found any.

The ridges on the other side of the valley were thickly wooded with white and red oak, basswood, pine, cherry, and hickory—a disorderly parade of veterans, leaning toward one another or away, carrying their fire scars and broken limbs with pride, telling their stories over and over. Young trees struggled for their share of light. In isolated patches, walnuts clustered. An antisocial tree, the walnut mingles only with its own kind.

In the fall, we gathered acorns and walnuts, and as we wandered in the woods we buried them in likely places, just as the squirrels have always done. In the spring, we planted seedlings— oak, maple, white ash—and watched for their new growth with the excitement of a doting grandmother.

Laird always says I married him for the valley. And I deny it, knowing all the while that within the complex intertwining webs that bind us, there is a fiber of truth in what he says. Here in this small slice of Wisconsin, I feel a sense of being truly at home.

The White Pine

Come into the forest with me. Walk softly and inhale the breath of the trees. These are Charles Baudelaire's living pillars. Close your eyes and listen; they have so much to say. Let them comfort you with their sighs, their patience. Anchored deeply in the forest floor, they share infrequent sunbeams. Notice the shadowy interstices, thick with drifting motes and spores. Regeneration is happening as you watch.

Let me introduce you to this white pine. *Pinus strobus Linnaeus* can be identified by its bundles of five long needles. The gentlest of the pines, its bark is smooth slate gray, but it weeps sticky resin where twigs have snapped or birds have drilled holes looking for insects. The resin, which won't wash off easily, discourages tree hugging.

This pine was here before Wisconsin was a state, before our grandparents and great grandparents were born. In 1832, when the surveyor came through with his chains and his notebook, it might have been a tiny sprout, not big enough for him to notice. The lead miners who roamed the area with their picks and shovels, gouging out pits and leaving piles of rock and clay, were more interested in what was beneath the land. They established diggings and built smelting furnaces fired with wood—good hard oak, which was abundant. They would not have noticed a green puff of pine needles poking up among the oak leaves, sending its delicate leader each year up and up.

And so it grew, watching the miners leave when the meager minerals gave out, their huts and smelting furnace eventually collapsing in rubble. It witnessed the farmer who came next, pasturing a few cows to supply the village of Ridgeway cheese factories with milk and ripping up the prairie plants to plow the soil for grain. The pine was in nobody's way; it was uphill from the bottomlands, hidden among the aspen clumps and scattered oaks, clutching the sandstone outcroppings. The farmer didn't hack it off. Wildfires had spared it. The grazing cows and white-tailed deer, so fond of tender pine, somehow overlooked it.

The farmer left many decades ago. Access to the valley was difficult, and the thin soil of the fields wouldn't support a family. The tree enjoyed long seasons of solitude when only the hunters came—until we arrived, the curious ones, who walk the paths doing no damage, trying to listen and to learn its secrets. Many generations of birds have hidden or nested in its branches—barred owls, towhees, finches. Perhaps it hosted a flock of passenger pigeons before they met extinction. I'd like to think so.

Each year, its needles turn yellow, then cinnamon-tawny, and drop, contradicting the description "evergreen." But so subtle is its molting, shedding a few needles at a time as it grows new ones, that we have the illusion of green continuity. Each year, too, it drops its long cones to roll and nestle in the spongy earth. The seeds embedded in the cone might sprout and, if the seedling finds a fortunate slice of sunlight, it will start another generation.

The pine grows another foot in height each year—and with enough light and rain, sometimes more. And perhaps an inch in girth, although at this age the growth slows. A half inch surely. If this were 150 years ago, when logging in Wisconsin was at its peak, this pine would be a treasure—first for ship masts, and then for houses.

It would be felled and sawed into lumber. Today, there is little demand for pine, and it would cost more to cut and haul it away than a logger would get in return. And so I will continue to admire it, to listen to its voices in the wind. Because this is what I do.

Forest Management Plan

The surveyor's notes suggested that the oaks are the real owners of this land. Oaks were dominant because they survived the frequent fires that occurred over several centuries. Some of the fires were natural—caused by lightning strikes—while other blazes were set by the Indians to clear the brush for hunting. The flames apparently spared the north slopes where the white pine ruled.

Fires can be a natural and important part of the life cycle of a forest. But I still wonder, if not for its effects, which species might be dominant on our land? As nonscientists with human life spans, we knew we would not be able to answer our questions by recording decades of observations or changes in something as long-lived as trees. We needed to learn more about their lives and whether they needed our attention.

We discovered early and often, as we tried to manage our land, that the Wisconsin Department of Natural Resources was a wonderfully conceived and operated government agency. We were familiar with Gaylord Nelson and George Meyer, and we were always pleased to read the *Wisconsin Natural Resources* magazine published by the DNR and learn what was being done to protect our beautiful Wisconsin natural environment. Alas, as politics changed over the years under new governors, budgets were cut, and shifts in management drove many wonderful people to leave the department.

From the first time we set foot on our land, we had occasional visits from staff of various branches of the DNR. I remember the first meeting with Mark Martin and Doris Ruesch, from the Bureau of Endangered Resources, who were pleased to hear of our restoration plans and offered advice—suggestions, booklets, names of experts, information on possible grants. They also told us that our land was part of a larger area designated by the DNR as the Ridgeway Pines, which consisted of about one thousand acres of Driftless Area land, notable for its geology and vegetation. The DNR wanted to own the land, including our small parcel, and make it available to the public as a State Natural Area.

"You mean like a public park?" I asked, alarmed. "Do we have a choice?" They assured me that it had been listed as a top priority area for years, and as parts of the land became available, the DNR would offer to purchase them. In the meantime, we had nothing to worry about. "Well, you'll never see *us* selling *this* land," I declared, with naive certainty. And they smiled.

These were the years when we attended workshops being put on by the DNR and by another of our favorite groups, the Prairie Enthusiasts, as well as meetings of the Wisconsin Woodland Owners Association. We learned much valuable information on invasive species and prairie management and met many dedicated and knowledgeable people at these events.

We probably first became familiar with the DNR's Managed Forest Law at one of these early workshops. Although we had been concentrating our efforts on the prairie, the truth was that much of our land—probably 90 percent—was forested. For sheer beauty, I revered the oak ridges and the high pine relict for walking through and admiring, but I hadn't given much thought to whether they needed our attention.

I inquired further and got a copy of the 1985 Managed Forest Law, which described a landowner incentive program that encouraged sustainable forestry on private woodland. The purpose of the Managed Forest Law was to encourage sound forestry practices, "which consider the objectives of the individual property owner, forest aesthetics, wildlife habitat, erosion control, protection of endangered or threatened plants and animals, and compatible recreational activities." In exchange for following such practices, the landowner paid reduced property taxes.

It sounded good to us, so we worked with a forester who drew up a plan for our land, with recommendations for removal of diseased or crowded trees and some harvesting of older oaks to allow the younger trees to grow and develop. All of this was to take place over twenty-five to fifty years. The prairie was also mentioned in the plan, with the objective "to maintain and restore prairie ecosystem with burning and mowing," which we were already doing. We enthusiastically signed on, starting in the year 1996.

During the early years we came to know the Iowa County foresters who would be working with us and found them to be helpful and patient as we tried to follow the requirements of the plan. In 1999, they encouraged us to do an "improvement harvest" of "dead, dying, damaged, defective, and deformed trees." (Foresters, I thought, seemed enamored of "d" adjectives!)

I knew that the DNR was not popular in many parts of the state because of the various restrictions on hunting, fishing, and other activities that landowners considered their God-given rights, but we were always grateful for their assistance.

The foresters came out to mark trees for removal, including some that I was very fond of. They wanted to remove some perfectly good sugar maples that flaunt their colors in the fall, as well as some wild cherry and basswood. In the confrontation that ensued, I argued, "But this is our woods. Our goal is a healthy and diverse forest, managed for wildlife and aesthetics."

"Aesthetics is a subjective thing," countered the forester with a frown. Indeed, it was. Nevertheless, it was our land, and

we wanted our
preferred aesthet-
ics to outweigh
theirs. The sugar
maples and bass-
wood would stay,
as well as some
of the aspen. The
elms would die of
their own accord,
but it was import-
ant to keep them from
falling on other trees.

As we planned the har-
vest, we worried about the damage that would be done to our forest
by logging equipment. We scheduled the cutting to take place in
the winter when the ground was frozen to minimize damage and
avoid nesting season.

We had recently joined yet another group, this one dedicated
to sustainable timber management. This involved removing less
desirable timber, drying it to add value, taking advantage of
markets that could use it, and then replanting to replace it with
higher-quality timber. Forester Jim Birkemeier talked to the
group about forming a cooperative to manage our own logging
process rather than putting it in the hands of some possibly un-
scrupulous timber scalper. With other friends and landowners, I
joined the group and served on the board. We even had a kiln in
Lone Rock and held monthly meetings to discuss this new way
of harvesting trees. At one or another meeting of the "Sustainable
Woods Cooperative," we learned about the option of using horses
to drag out the trees instead of mechanical equipment, and of
course that was also appealing.

David and Shelley, who had moved north into Amish territory, recommended an Amish logger who would be happy to do the job for us. We had to pay for his and the horses' transportation, but it still seemed worth it to us. They camped overnight one cold winter and, following the sustainable plan, took out the older or defective oaks that had been marked. The logs were stacked beside the path. We then had to find a trucker who would carry them up to the top of our tortuous driveway, a few at a time, and pile them by side of the road, where yet another truck could pick them up and deliver them in several loads to the sawmill to get milled and dried. As I recall, we then paid the DNR a percentage.

As we totaled up the proceeds on our timber sale, we discovered we were in the red by about twelve hundred dollars and not eager to do any more logging. We did pursue grants for forest improvement and hired help to remove invasive growth—mainly honeysuckle and multiflora rose. But as the managed forest plan did not require us to do further cutting for another twenty years, we did no further harvests.

Planting the Red Oaks

In January one year, a flyer arrived in the mail advertising native trees for sale at low prices by the Sauk County Conservation Department. My mind was jolted from its January torpor into a frenzy of anticipation. Outside, the wind gusted, stirring up some new-spilled flakes of snow, breathing its icy warnings around the rattling window frames. I had been staring out at the patterns of tree branches, stark against the white sky, and writing poems about trees.

I read the list of trees and their descriptions, visualizing the shape of the oak, the crimson leaves of the sugar maple. In my mind, they were tall and stately.

The previous year I had ordered one hundred trees from the same outfit. When the trees arrived, we were notified to come pick them up in Reedsburg, about fifty miles away. I took Laird's Jeep and cleared out the back to make lots of room for my new trees. After circling the city, unable to find the county landfill where they were being distributed, I finally pulled up at the metal shed.

"I've come for my trees," I said, with barely repressed excitement.

A very friendly bald man with a generous paunch handed me a paper sack, about the size of a grocery bag but not so heavy.

"Is this all?" I peered in at the miniatures, looking for all the world like bundles of Fourth of July sparklers.

On my way back to the valley with my precious, if meager, cargo, I got a speeding ticket for 160 dollars, so the cost of each tree sprig immediately escalated.

This year I would not be so foolish. I knew where the landfill was, I would anticipate small seedlings, and I would learn to be patient. Trees, after all, are the ultimate lesson in patience.

Now it was another January, and I was contemplating my tree order. Red and white oaks for sure, to replace the ones that were harvested. And maybe some green ash this year instead of the white, although the white had done well. Or at least, they had done well until the deer nibbled the tops off them. So maybe this year I would order tree tubes as well, to protect them against the deer. If I ordered tree tubes, I would need stakes and twist ties to anchor them. The order grew.

The flyer offered Chinese chestnut, and I wondered how this could be considered native. I knew that all native chestnut trees had died and that breeders had been trying to develop a disease-resistant strain by crossing them with Chinese chestnuts. Maybe they had succeeded. Wouldn't it be fun to have the first successful chestnut trees in Iowa County? I marked the box for twenty-five chestnuts, the smallest number you could order of each species. My order was now up to one hundred. That's how many I got last year, and since they arrived soon after my knee surgery, I had to send out an SOS for friends to help me plant. We had a very successful tree-planting party, and I planned to organize the same event again. At least I thought it had been successful. Had my friends agreed? We'd be able to tell by how many showed up for a repeat.

I made arrangements to go away with three friends for a writers' retreat at the end of April and prayed that the trees would not arrive before the trip. With bare roots, they would need to go into the ground as soon as possible. Alas, the notification arrived, with a pickup date two days before I was to leave town, and I couldn't cancel my plans to attend the retreat.

Laird went with me to pick them up this time and pointed out that it took him more than a half tank of gas to get to Reedsburg and back, that gas was really high right then, and that this expense needed to be factored into the cost of the trees. At least we didn't get a ticket. And even with the gas, the trees averaged out to only a few cents apiece. In a mere two hundred years they would be worth immensely more.

The two of us had just one day to get as many planted as we could. We wrapped the other trees in damp newspaper and put them in buckets in the cool basement of the cabin. They would wait, dark and still, patiently holding their buds and juices until we told them it was time.

We arrived at the cabin by ten in the morning for planting. It was a breathtakingly lovely day, the new foliage still unfolding in subtle pastels—like cloud puffs along the stream bank. I inhaled the sweetness and registered the clamor of birds, and then I focused on the work to be done. I was driven to get those trees into the ground. I decided to start with the red oaks, which were the largest of the seedlings—already almost two feet tall, branched and sturdy. They would need the five-foot stakes and tree tubes and would go on the dry ridges where the loggers had removed their predecessors.

Laird was being sweetly, patiently cooperative, although I knew that this was not how he would have preferred to spend the day. Not that he would rather have played golf or gone to a ballpark, but he would have dearly loved to sit on the deck and read, watch the birds, and live out those dreams that we prattled about.

We started up the slope back of the cabin, where it got progressively steeper. The previous spring, the loggers had done a lot of cutting here, calling it timber stand improvement. They had sliced off dozens of giant honeysuckle, warty cherry trees, and elms, leaving them in big snarly piles. Gooseberry, blackberry, and prickly ash already dominated the undergrowth. Why is it the invasive species come so well armed to snag and mutilate? Just struggling through this mess was a rigorous task, and we were each carrying tools: shovels, clippers, a bucket of water with ten red oak seedlings, gloves, stakes, tree tubes, tape. We slid and tripped as we looked for passageways through this obstacle course. And sometimes there were none, so we backed down to start another way.

I had already been up here once that morning, scouting out good sites and putting red flags where I wanted the trees to go. Now we dug. Sometimes we were lucky and hit rich deep earth. More often, the shovel hit rock, and we would try a different spot, and maybe again. The rock outcroppings up here are St. Peter sandstone, named for deposits found along the then-named St. Peter River (now Minnesota River). I like to think that these are the old foundations of cabins built by the lead miners back in the 1820s and 1830s. If I were a miner looking for a place to put a cabin, what could be better than this high hillside that faces the length of the valley, offering a view in front and protection from behind?

From up there, I felt like a bird looking down on the cabin roof, out to the sky, the fields, the long ridges to east and west. And I could see how many trees there already were. When my son David came one spring to help us plant trees, he looked around and said, "Mom, don't you think this is a little overkill?" But I explained about the good trees and the bad trees and about the necessity for replanting after harvest. He too was patient with my passions. Patient and bemused.

Laird dug holes about six inches deep and maybe ten inches wide, depending on the shape of the root cluster. We poured in water and placed the seedling upright. They were rough and sturdy little trees, holding within their stalks the possibility of majesty. Down on my knees, I crumbled the dark earth clods so that the soil would cradle the roots and fill in around them with its protecting, nurturing molecules. We filled each hole and tamped it down. Then Laird pounded in a stake, and we slid the plastic tube over the tree, squeezing the little branches together so they would fit. He secured the tube with a strip of foam-backed tape. The tube was about three feet taller than the tree, so it would be a few years before the deer could get at it. It was translucent and drilled with air holes and so that light would get in. I peered down from the top at my new oak and thought it seemed a little crowded, but thankfully, claustrophobia has never been known to be a problem for trees.

At one point we disturbed a chickadee nest. I didn't see it, but when I tossed an old branch to one side, all at once they were around us—about four angry chickadees, perched on branches and "dee-dee-deeing" loudly, so small and so incensed. I apologized and sincerely hoped I had not done actual mayhem to their prospective families. I do love chickadees, so merry and insouciant. I would have liked to tell them that I was thinking only of their futures—of new perching and shelter opportunities. But these birds and these trees would never have time to become acquainted. The birds would be long gone before the trees—if they survived—would be released from their tubes to reach out spindly branches. With trees, you must learn to think in longer time spans.

This bothered Laird, who confessed to me in the evening over dinner that he really didn't enjoy the tree planting. We were both stiff and creaky. "I keep thinking I'll never even see these trees grow up," he said. "I'll look out the window and not notice them. All this work, and it won't even make a difference."

If I had not been so tired, I might have tried to tell him why it did make a difference.

Tree Hugger Meets Farmer

The valley, surrounded as it is by ridges on all sides, imparted a heady feeling of isolation akin to the childlike euphoria of finding the secret garden, the tree fort. It offered escape from the small frantic dailiness we imposed on ourselves and from the larger, incendiary world of shopping malls and talk shows. We wandered the land, watched the birds, planted and burned the prairie, improved the woods. Unless we turned on the radio—which we rarely did—we were alone.

And yet, geographically we were not as isolated as we liked to pretend. One white sliver of the Ridgeway water tower peered above the pines at the far end of the valley. Trucks on the highway two miles away roared and rumbled when the breeze was from the south. We could hear a tractor in the distance, breaking up the black clods of a spring field; an occasional chain saw split the tranquility.

And once in a while we heard the deep, impassioned "maauw" of a cow, one of the handful that were pastured on neighboring land.

One Saturday when we drove down, we noticed large footprints in the drive. Big, round footprints. And then the unmistakable odor of cow manure.

Sure enough, we had been invaded by a herd of large bovines, who had trampled around in the soft spring earth, making muddy craters up and down around the cabin, as though they were curious and wanted to see in. They had walked through the sandbox, knocked over the grill and the furniture, and left an amazing output of still-fresh cowsplat every few inches. There wasn't a path anywhere that they hadn't marked with their presence.

My first thought was for the three acres of young trees we had just planted across the stream. Had they gotten that far? Where had they come from, and were they still here? And how would we tell them to please leave?

I started to track them down along the stream and could see by the gouged and eroded stream banks where they had marched across, several times. At that moment I hated cows, their stupidity and destructiveness, and their large, post hole–digging feet.

After we crossed the stream on a log, we could see a cow path that looked like the old Chisholm Trail marching straight toward my baby trees. It looked like the cows had performed some bovine schottische dance, stepping back and forth across my saplings. I had to turn and leave, my heart heavy, the cost of the trees and labor like a sour lump in the back of my throat.

It took a number of phone calls to find out whose cows they were, and when I finally reached the farmer, he didn't have any idea how they had gotten onto our land. He rented a pasture from people whose land shared a short border with ours. Perhaps they'd come through there. Perhaps it was even our fence that was down! In any event, he'd gotten them out. And didn't want, he said, any "unpleasantness." I'd already left a number of messages on a number of answering machines, and they could easily be called unpleasant. I felt unpleasant. If I were a master gardener whose prize rose garden had been savaged, I could not have felt more unpleasant.

We agreed to meet with the farmer and talk about damages. But first, I had to get a better count of damaged trees. And so I spent an afternoon tramping through old brush piles and muddy paths seeking out and counting the infant trees, my scrawny seedlings, the promise of tomorrow's forest. In truth, only a few were knocked over, but I had to ensure that it didn't happen again.

We met then, face to face. Joe, the dairy farmer, and I, the tree hugger, shook hands. He seemed about seven feet tall, with arms and shoulders like oak branches. If we'd been in a western, he would have been booted and spurred, with a six-gun at his hip. His brown eyes were quizzical, behind thick glasses. We circled each other uncertainly in the farmyard beside his enormous blue barn, where six hundred cows munched at their stanchions, while machines sucked their udders dry. The roar from an air compressor or ventilator made it hard to talk. My righteous indignation was subsiding like a failed meringue.

"What I want is to be sure they don't get on our land again," I said. He shrugged, not unpleasantly. What does this person want? he might have been thinking.

"It turns out not many of the trees were actually damaged," I said, reassuringly.

"How much is a tree worth?" he asked. How much a tree is worth, to me, is incalculable. But I understood that he was really asking how much money we'd lost.

"I paid about a dollar-fifty a tree," I said, "with labor."

"Get cost-sharing money for that?" he asked. He's familiar with the Forest Landowner Grant, of course.

"Some," I acknowledged, feeling my case disintegrate.

"Critters gonna get some anyhow," he said. "How you gonna keep deer off 'em?"

He had me there.

"But—but your cows made big footprints all over my prairie!" I said, indignantly. "They eroded the stream banks. They probably brought in invasive . . . uh, weed seeds into my prairie!"

He raised his eyebrows. He didn't need to say anything. I felt like I had complained about noise from the wind, or gravel on the road.

"What's this stuff about prairies anyhow?" he asked, finally, as the gulf between us yawned. "My grandfather started farming here one hundred and fifty years ago. Now they're puttin' this good farmland into prairies!" He said the word as if I'd proposed planting poison ivy.

I shuffled my feet. "Yeah. Well. We just want it how it used to be. You know, before it was plowed. The native grasses and forbs, you know. We want to restore the prairie that used to be here."

In his eyes I saw the twinkle that said he knew he was talking to a crazy person. We shook hands again. He handed me a newspaper with an ad for a fence maker, and then we parted. I understood him, but I doubted that he would ever understand me.

Snowshoeing to the Cabin

I was scared, but it was something I had to do. I hadn't been to the cabin for three weeks, and I kept worrying about the birds, picturing them flying to the feeders and away again, hungry and disappointed.

We'd had two generous snowfalls and a couple of fill-ins in less than a week. Here at home, the snow measured eighteen inches on the back deck. The drive to the valley was about thirty-five miles along a major highway. Still, the most recent snowfall had lasted all the previous day, and the radio said plenty of cars were still in ditches.

Navigating the long, unplowed driveway wasn't an option, of course; there were even some questions about whether Rosy Lane would be plowed. Nevertheless, I decided to go. I got out my snowshoes and put together a backpack of essentials, with Laird's assistance. He wanted to go along, but his doctor had advised against it after a recent knee operation.

I carried an apple, a bottle of water, and plenty of warm clothes. I would have to stop at the co-op and replenish the bird food supply but would only be able to carry whatever the backpack could hold. I put in the snowshoes and poles, a snow shovel in case the car got stuck, and, of course, the cell phone in case I needed to call for help.

The day was perfect, the sky as deep blue as mountain pools, sunshine enough to make a blinding glare across the crystal landscape. I headed west on the highway, somewhat more slowly than usual and leery of the big trucks in the snow-slick passing lane.

In a pristine field, a snowmobile had left one track, opening up access to the cornfield below, and the track was lined with blackbirds, like a long obsidian necklace.

Trees steepled the horizon, outlined in white. Each one carried several inches on every branch and twig, letting it go in a puff of breeze and whirl of powder. Blue shadows curved along the fields. Each wooden fencepost wore a beret, and the round loaves of hay were like igloos. The Angus cattle made black silhouettes on a white page.

I turned off on County Highway HHH and put the car in four-wheel drive, though the roads so far had been passable. Iowa County snowplows had been diligent. Rosy Lane was sanded at the uphill turn. But along the stretch by our driveway, the snowbank stood about two feet high where the plow had piled it, leaving no place to park the car. Continuing to the next driveway, I could see it was equally piled. At the goat farm across the road, there was no sign of life. Two trucks were parked and snow covered, but the driveway hadn't been plowed, and there weren't even any footprints to tell me if anyone was at home.

I went down Fred's Lane, thinking the family there might be home and let me park in their extra driveway, but I found no sign of access there either. They must have stayed in Madison. I turned back to Rosy Lane, realizing there was no help for it. I got out and carved a parking place out of the two-foot hardpack the plow had left. My back complained, but I didn't listen. Finally, I was able to nudge the car at least halfway off the road.

It was time to gear up for the trek downhill. I felt exhilarated, like a bold adventuress in the northland, heading across the glacier to rescue someone trapped and needy. I put on the snowshoes, swearing a little as my hat fell off in the snow, my glasses fogged up, and my scarf kept tangling with the damnably complicated bindings. Finally the shoes felt tight enough. Made of light aluminum, once on, they proved very satisfactory. I put on my pack and walked the several yards to the top of the driveway. The chain that acted as a perfunctory gate was completely covered with snow, so I stepped over. Immediately I sank ten inches into the fluffy stuff and wallowed for a few steps before I remembered my camera, back in the car. After retrieving the camera, a secondary but important purpose of the trip, at last I was on my way.

The snow was so deep that I sank eight to ten inches with each step, despite the wide snowshoes. However, it was so light and weightless that it didn't feel strenuous. The snowshoes were lightweight and easy, and I loved them with the fondness we have for simple things that work. Walking in boots would have been impossible.

Soon I was within the arms of the woods, part of a bold woodcut of black and white. Awed and gaping, I snapped pictures, knowing it would be difficult to capture this snowy wonderland on film but unable to resist. Dead trees had taken on new personae, their branches sinuous and twisted in ways I had never noticed before. The sun flashed as I turned the first hairpin corner and entered blue shadow. The deer trails looked almost like ski tracks, and I used them, grateful for any shallower trail. A hawk flew away noisily. Otherwise it was perfectly still.

At the bottom of the long decline, the cottonwood was well cloaked. It was easy to see how many branches it had lost in the last few years. We had noticed that it had very little foliage that year, so its days seemed to be numbered. It would probably come down soon, but not just yet, I hoped, and hurried past. I began to feel the pull of muscles in my upper thighs and hoped they were taking the brunt of the lifting, not my bad knees. As I shuffled the last few hundred yards I looked eagerly ahead for the cabin. Always in the back of my mind was the specter of vandals, since they used to visit occasionally in the early years. It would be a simple thing to smash a glass door and get inside, ransacking, letting in snow and squirrels. Laird didn't like to hear my neurotic fantasies, so I kept them to myself.

Finally, there ahead was the cabin, serene and snow-blanketed. Before I could take off the snowshoes and go in, I needed to unload birdseed into the feeders. On the one in front, two pitiful chickadees peered inside as if they couldn't believe the emptiness. I told them to be patient and that I would be there in a minute. I lowered the feeder on its pulley and removed the snow and ice covering. The bag I brought just filled up the container. There would be enough left in the basement for the other ones. I was barely back to the cabin before the first chickadee made his approach. What would they have done if I hadn't come? People who know more about birds than I do reassure me that they would get along without help, but I chose to help anyhow.

The sun was warm on the deck and had melted most of the snow there, so I flailed up the steps to the picnic table and sat down to remove the snowshoes. The valley was quiet, a watercolor in black and white, undisturbed except for its real owners, the big and little critters. Squirrels had obviously been playing on and under the trees, and deer tracks were everywhere. I unlocked the door and breathed in the woodsmoke smell, sighing with pleasure. All was well, everything as we had left it.

My first task was to light a fire. Although I felt overheated from the trek down, my breath was coming out in misty puffs inside the cabin, where the temperature was about twenty-five degrees. I put in paper and kindling and a couple of logs and got a nice little blaze roaring, pulled the couch up close, and took off my boots and gloves to let warm air thaw me and them. I heated up a bowl of hot gumbo, ate my apple, drank some water, and wrote a few lines in the journal.

It was clear that the fire was not going to heat up the whole cabin, and I would not want to hang around too long with freezing fingers. I still had to fill the other feeders and take photos. In the back of the cabin, up above the stone retaining wall, was the big feeder. I retrieved the bag of seed from the basement and carried the bag and scoop onto the deck, put the snowshoes back on, and tried to figure how to clamber up the wall in my snowshoes. I shuffled to the far end, where it was only about a foot high, and stepped up, only to catch my shoes under some black raspberry bushes and fall flat on my face. Next spring I would have to remember to remove those bushes.

On my feet again, I opened the lid of the big feeder and poured many scoopfuls in, hoping this would hold the birds for the week or so till I could return. I also had brought a suet ball to hang from the hook on the oak branch, but it turned out the hook—placed by Laird—was too high for me to reach. With nothing to stand on, and not wanting to go back down to the basement for a ladder, I piled and packed the snow until I had a viable platform to step up on. From there I could almost reach the hook. I pulled the loop of string up straight, groped for the hook, and, at last, slid it on.

While I was there, I wanted to get some pictures. I headed out across my sleeping prairie toward the stream, frozen in its voluptuously curved banks, the elegance of dried weeds waving above, and took some shots of the cabin from this distance. Beautiful! Unfortunately, my camera jammed at this point, possibly from the cold, and the next six or eight photos didn't turn out. The curse of the amateur photographer.

It was time to head uphill. As the well-fed birds happily swooped and twittered, I pulled on the pack, now considerably lighter, and started back in my own tracks. I was amused to see that while I had been puttering around, some very quiet deer had taken the opportunity to walk in my tracks as I walked in theirs. In every snowshoe oval was a perfectly placed hoofprint. Where were they? I longed to see a hint of tan fur, a flashing tail.

It was a long and weary walk uphill, but I was so glad I had done this. If nothing else, I proved to myself that I could. This gives me more sense of accomplishment than polishing the furniture or cleaning out closets. Oh, yes!

The Later Years

A conservationist is one who is humbly aware that with each stroke he is writing his signature on the face of his land.
—ALDO LEOPOLD, *A SAND COUNTY ALMANAC*

The New Cabin

For ten years, from 1988 until 1998, the cabin and the valley were the dominant obsession in our lives. During our workweek, we dreamed and plotted and planned, and on Saturday morning we loaded up the car and drove forty-five minutes west, to another world. Along with relatives, friends and neighbors, scientists and DNR representatives, we explored, mowed, burned, clipped, and planted—thrilling to each new discovery and each success, disheartened by the frequent failures. Nearly every visit was recorded in the journals we kept faithfully, and most of the entries recorded joy and amazement. I was frequently inspired to write poems, many of which found a place in publications or in my own poetry books.

We continued to attend conferences of groups such as the Prairie Enthusiasts, benefited from lectures and workshops, and met many wonderful and knowledgeable people who loved and cared for their land, as we were trying to do. We joined a group of landowners from the Driftless Area (mainly Iowa County) who were equally involved in restoration. From them we learned additional skills and visited each other's land to appreciate successes. We invited them to our land and shared tools, knowledge, and labor. We assisted each other on burns. We named our group the OWLS, or Older and Wiser Land Stewards.

And so the years went by, and mingled among the journal

entries were complaints about the cabin. What had seemed charming and rustic in the early years now became a chore. We frequently invited friends out, and managing a meal in our substandard kitchen was an ordeal. Carpenter ants were eating the wood siding, the basement was leaking, and mice continued to sneak in. Sleeping on mattresses on the deck had lost some of its charm.

In 1998 we began talking about how to make the cabin more comfortable—for us and for the many visitors. We had celebrated our first grandchild and envisioned introducing him to all the wonders we had discovered at our valley hideaway. And then we always came up against the lack of running water and toilet facilities. At first we talked about enlarging or remodeling, and invited several contractors to visit and talk. They pointed out the cracked and decaying foundation of the cabin and shook their heads at the difficult driveway.

As the year 2000 loomed, we both planned retirement from our jobs—Laird from teaching math at the local technical college, and me from my comfortable part-time position as assistant to the dean of letters and science at UW–Madison. The time seemed right for a change in several ways: the end of millennium, the start of Social Security. All the signs were there.

Don Richards, an architect friend whom I had met at my previous job, said he would be interested in helping us design a new cabin. He and his wife had been frequent visitors to the valley and understood our passion, as well as our problems. He came up with a set of plans for a new cabin that matched our ideas beautifully: one large main room with a bedroom and bathroom nook to one side, and a kitchen on the other, with back windows looking out on the oak savanna hill behind. Above would be a loft with space for children, or hardy hunters, to sleep. From the large front windows and sliding doors in the main room, we would have a view of the valley and access to a large roofed deck, overlooking the prairie and ridges in front.

We found a contractor, Rick Hansen, who lived in the area and who didn't balk at the driveway. We immediately liked him, we signed some papers, and before we knew it, things started happening fast!

I had to go before the Ridgeway Town Board to ask for a variance. If we were planning a full-time habitation, we were required to do the major driveway improvement that we wanted to avoid. If we could show that the new cabin would fit the same footprint as the old and was only a weekend retreat, we wouldn't have to do this. I was able to convince them.

The next question was whether we would be able to add electricity. This was settled when we found out how much it would cost to run a line all the way down and how many trees we would lose. Losing trees always tipped the scale for me. We decided we would manage with gas power for lights, stove, and refrigerator. This was probably a poor decision, in the long run. With more amenities, we might have been able to extend our stewardship longer.

We removed everything of value and peeled off and disposed of the asphalt roof. One day while we were both still in our offices, the contractor demolished the old shack. And the next time we arrived, a giant hole yawned.

The new cabin was a post-and-beam construction, meaning that it was put together a little like Lincoln Logs. The contractor had found Douglas fir beams that were being sold secondhand from the demolition of Chicago factories. They were a beautiful tawny gold color.

We were on site often as the cabin took shape, and we made many extra trips to prime the siding, on both sides, and then to put the finish coat on—the color of tree trunks. Since we were

both still working, though, we juggled several urgent matters—
such as the approvals of the septic system, new well, and propane tank—from our office phones. The pouring of the new
concrete basement, when the cement truck nearly careened off
the driveway and down a gully, was a particularly harrowing day!

The cabin was completed in spring of 2000, and in May we
held a family reunion to celebrate. All three of my sons were there,
from California and Ohio, with two wives and two grandchildren.
Laird's sister, Jan, also attended with her daughter, son-in-law,
and one grandchild, as well as Laird's sister-in-law, Meg, and her
two boys. We wanted to encourage them all to feel ownership
for the valley and to use the cabin as they wished. The Marshall
part of the family honored their parents or grandparents, and it
was a fine celebration. Laird had wisely put up a plastic fencing
around the deck (called a "Plunge-No-More,") so the little ones
wouldn't tumble off.

Of course, "completed" is a bit of an exaggeration. Many tasks
remained for us to finish, and we continued to putter for years.

The loyal deer hunters, too, gave us a hand frequently, and in return they enjoyed their two weeks of hunting season in the new cabin. Although we had no less work to do, the new cabin was living up to our dreams. One happy housewarming gift was from our amazingly clever friend, Ulrich, who designed and built a bed for us that rolled out onto the deck for sleeping—and watching the stars, and listening to the owls.

We purchased a new efficient wood stove for heating and a secondhand gas stove for cooking. From an old building on campus that was being remodeled, I scavenged a marble sink for the bathroom, and my cousin David crafted a beautiful mirror to go over it. The double kitchen sink was a relic from Laird's grandparents, as were the antique dining table and chairs. It was also lovely to have a flush toilet and shower and sink in the bathroom, running water in the kitchen, a gas refrigerator, and plentiful cabinet space. The roomy and dry basement under the cabin held tools—burn equipment, saws, and axes—as well as the water tank, bags of seed, and various other equipment.

Now I could sit at my desk in the new cabin, as I had often imagined myself. My less than perfect view—over the new septic system to the tractor shed—seemed perfect to me, framed as it was by gnarly bur oak and silver maple, with branches from the old apple tree reaching in from the right side, heavy with yellow-green golf-ball-sized apples.

I remember one sunny morning with a lively breeze when I pondered for a couple of minutes the many tasks that called to me insistently. Should I grade and seed the slope outside, where a contractor had just finished the retaining wall? Should I cut more honeysuckle, gooseberry, and prickly ash above the pump, where five or six young hazelnut trees were thriving?

The day before, I had finished grouting the fireplace tiles and cleaned off the extra grout as I went along, cursing myself continually for the mess of grout I hadn't cleaned last fall, which had now hardened into stone. How would I ever get it off? While I worked, we kept a brush fire going outside to burn construction scraps and great mounds of brush. It made me happy to get rid of the messes. Laird was agreeable to the fire, as the day was very still, overcast, and muggy. He did house chores, all the wonderful useful things I couldn't do: hung the toilet paper holder, wind chime, and bird feeder, and finished the bedroom shelf. How well we worked together, each to our own appointed task. What a fine time we were having!

Sunday on the Savanna

Sunday morning on the savanna behind the cabin, I was in my sanctuary. From the far end of the valley, behind high hills, I could hear the distant mellow ringing of church bells from Ridgeway. I was thankful not to have to respond. The faithful and the dutiful bless their god in their way, and I in mine. I would not want to miss this golden morning, pungent with earth and decay, sunlight shifting in the breeze. A few leaves drifted down, but green still predominated.

That morning we decided it was time to gather seeds of the purple hyssop. We'd been working on the savanna behind the cabin, approximately half an acre of steep hillside, for five years now. A savanna is an interface between woods and prairie, with scattered oak trees and specific plants adapted to this environment. We had planted this area with oaks some years back, and I was always pleased to see the young ones that survived and had outgrown their tree tubes. This area was once open. We have a photograph from the 1960s that shows a stand of wide-armed bur oaks with space between. But it had degenerated over the years into a jungle of gooseberry and prickly ash, honeysuckle and buckthorn, as well as young elm and cherry trees. We hired two young men who cleared brush and girdled non-oak trees, burned it that year and each fall since, and seeded with a mixture of savanna plants after each burn.

It was exciting to watch the progression. The first year, the tall grasses appeared, with wild rye grass and bottlebrush, that grass that looks just like its name, dominant. Also in the mix was a generous sprinkling of purple hyssop, a tall spiked plant with many tiny purple blossoms, and tall bellflower, which does not have bell-shaped flowers but flat, five-petaled flowerets, also strung on a tall stem. Over the years, we saw more and more welcome arrivals: woodland bromegrass and joe-pye weed, with its flat mass of fuzzy pale pink. Each new discovery was cause for celebration: zigzag goldenrod, tinker's weed with its orange berries, and many more.

But not all had gone as planned. Were we in charge? Of course not. The vigorous blackberry and black raspberry bramble, sizzled by fire each fall, came roaring back with increased vigor every spring and threatened to smother the entire area. The arching stalks planted their tips in the ground to create a veritable thorny wall and wrapped their vicious strands around our ankles, clawing at clothing and exposed skin.

In addition, the agrimony, Canada tick trefoil, sticktights, and others of their ilk, had gone to seed and insistently planted themselves on invading clothing. We armored ourselves against them with nylon chaps over our boots and brought along gloves, clippers, bags, and hats. My knee brace, cleverly constructed of Velcro strips to hold my knee in place, was an open invitation to every bur and sticky seedpod. After spending the first hour-long experience in picking them off, I had learned to wrap it in plastic.

We had at least three varieties of hyssop, short and tall purple and yellow, although my book listed only two: yellow giant (*Agastache nepetoides*) and purple giant (*Agastache scrofulariifolia*). Not a very pretty name for the purple, which definitely dominated. *Scrofulous*, according to the dictionary, is a term describing either a form of tuberculosis that affects the lymph glands or a morally degenerate person. How did this pretty plant get tagged with such a name?

The two varieties of purple hyssop, short and tall, early and late, had been ripening for some time now, and we plucked the flower heads as they turned from green to brown to harvest the seeds. If we were to wait until they were all brown, the finches would get there first. The difficult part was that once the petals dropped, we couldn't distinguish between yellow and purple. Since we promised purple hyssop seeds to Dane County naturalist Wayne Pauly, we began flagging the purple ones, tying bits of red markers while they were blooming, so we'd be sure and send him the right ones. Unfortunately the flags were often hard to spot amidst the bright red leaves of Virginia creeper.

But all challenges aside, it was a lovely morning to be right where we were, breathing in, listening, and making discoveries, plucking, clipping, and filling brown paper bags. Laird was much better at staying focused. I couldn't resist gathering the silky woodland bromegrass, bottlebrush, and rye. They were so satisfyingly eager to be harvested, easily slipping off between the fingers! I decided to fill two bags, one with savanna grasses and one with purple hyssop only. Then I noticed the clouds of woodland joe-pye—ready and waiting. In fact, if I didn't get them that day, the seeds would drop. I worried that when we burned in a month or so, the seeds might be lost. I wasn't sure if they could survive fires. So many unanswered questions swirled in my head. I got another bag and labeled it "savanna miscellany," since I had now managed to mix grasses and forbs (broad-leafed plants) randomly.

Tall clumps of one or another tempting plant were always just out of reach, up a steep rise, armored with bramble, which hid the rocks and logs beneath. I slipped and fell, twisting the already complaining knee, remembering that my physical therapist warned me to stay off uneven ground. Restoration is not for the weak or timid. The important thing is to maintain enough mobility to continue.

September mornings have a quiet simplicity that is so peaceful, so healing to the soul, after the frenetic noise and activity of spring and summer. I could hear each birdcall, separate from the cacophony of dozens more. One last phoebe called its name, a young one, I thought. I saw it perched this morning on the walnut tree, among the gently drifting yellow leaves and escaping walnuts. "FEE-bee, FEE-bee!" he announced, as though we needed to know his name.

A red-bellied woodpecker's noisy churr-churr-churr seemed to say, "I'm coming, I'm here, take note, and get out of my way." He had been frequenting the finch feeder with its tiny seeds and small holes, which didn't make a lot of sense, with his generous beak. We are hoping that our efforts at restoration will result in a return of the redheaded woodpecker, which we have not seen for some years.

All around us, things were dying. Many would return the following year, while some would not. The whip-poor-will and ruffed grouse, the woodcock and brown thrasher, no longer graced us with their presence, and we could only speculate that somewhere in their migration routes their habitat had been lost.

Despite the falls and brambles, despite the burs and confusion over what to pluck and what to mix, we had a satisfying morning and filled five grocery bags with somewhat differentiated seeds, ready to return either to this or to some other savanna. To anyone else, our scraggly hillside would have little meaning. To us, it was a work of love and creation.

Seeding the Prairie

Even with all the attention the new cabin still needed, plenty of outside chores needed to be done as well. The area in front of the cabin, where so much damage had been done during construction, would be my new prairie. The little creek that ran through it in the spring usually dried up by July. We ordered the appropriate prairie seeds from the Sauk County Conservation Department for what would be a damp, or mesic, prairie, and gathered seeds all fall. Every time we took a walk around the old field, we tweaked off ripe seed heads, the vital soul of each plant, and bagged and labeled them carefully.

The space, about a half acre or less, had been bare mud the previous spring and by fall had grown up in a nasty mixture of weeds, velvet leaf, Canada thistle, wild parsnip, stinging nettle, burdock, and dozens of other undesirables—undesirable because of their vicious or aggressive habits. They caused rashes or clung to clothing, and they proliferated madly, choking out the native prairie grasses and woodsy wildflowers.

I had finally accepted that Roundup had made the list of potentially health-threatening chemicals. If I had been able to, I would have pulled each plant out by hand. Unable to physically accomplish this, I enlisted the assistance of Roundup, but now protected by goggles, a respirator, and gloves.

After three separate sprayings with my backpack sprayer,

much of the area looked pretty dead. I raked lightly, since too much disruption would have just replanted the weed seeds. And I waited for the perfect day. November seemed right. Any earlier, and I would have newly sprouting annual weeds to contend with.

It was a gray day, thick with clumpy snowflakes, damp and quiet. I stopped at a friend's house to pick up a big bag of seeds—rosinweed, wild quinine, and rattlesnake master—and nearly got stuck in two inches of snow in his driveway. I wondered whether I'd be able to get back up our steep and twisty drive once I finished the day's planting. And what if I couldn't? The thought had always intrigued me. What a wonderful opportunity to be irresponsible! The cabin was stocked with lots of dry firewood and plenty of food in the cupboard.

As I turned down the driveway, I clicked off the radio as always and opened the car windows to let the smells and the silence seep in. Down and down, into the depths of the valley, into peace and solitude. Halfway down, a white-tailed deer bounded off into the pinewoods, and I tried not to think about the approach of hunting season.

The cabin was frigid, and unless I built a fire, I would not want to tarry. Some obligation was dragging me back to town by mid-afternoon, so I decided against the fire, put on another layer of clothes, and went down to the basement to prepare the seeds I had gathered, to add to the ones from my friend. Why did I label each bag so carefully, I asked myself, as I dumped them all together in a bucket and added a generous amount of damp sand from the grandkids' sandbox. Well, next spring, I'd at least have a record of what I planted, since it would be difficult to identify some of them till they bloomed.

The ground was squishy to walk on, bare in some places and slush-covered in others. I stirred the seeds and sand thoroughly with my bare hand and, starting at the far corner of the area, walked back and forth, sprinkling handfuls thinly over the uneven soil. Since the creek might flood its banks in spring, I didn't bother to waste much seed close to it. I'd love to have along its twists and turns Indian paintbrush, Turk's-cap lilies, or tiny swamp iris, but I would wait to see how well the creek followed its new course, which had been altered by the construction project.

I ran short of seed as I got to the last few hundred feet, so I gathered another bagful from the old field, just to fill in the gaps. Indian grass and liatris still waved their seed heads among the masses of sere goldenrod, as did bush clover, mint, and gray-headed coneflower. When they too had been dispersed, I tramped over the whole planting in my rubber boots, stomping the seeds down into the surface, away from marauding juncos, chickadees, and turkeys, although probably not out of reach of the field mice and little creeping voles. Nature would take over now, and most of my seed would probably be lost, but some would survive.

The snow thickened again, great wet snowballs from the sky. I turned my face up and caught a few flakes on my tongue, like I did as a child. I had a few more chores to do before I left. I spent a half hour or so constructing a giant chicken wire tube to surround the little apple tree we planted for our grandson Sam, who had learned to love the valley. The chicken wire was unwieldy, stubborn. It grabbed my jacket, scratched my hand. My frozen fingers dropped the pliers, and I was saying lots of words I wouldn't want Sam to hear. At last the tree was encircled, and I pounded three stakes through the wire and into the ground to secure it. It should keep the deer from nibbling off the tender twigs come spring.

Next I headed for the bend in the main creek, where a short log end had blocked passage. With a shovel I dug out the debris that had accumulated around it. The blockage was diverting the water, threatening to carve away the bank where a particularly nice clump of hazelnut was clinging. A few salmon-colored leaves still fluttered on its stalks. I had been meaning to shore up the hazelnut for weeks. I would not have wanted to lose it in the spring torrent.

Now, as I toted my shovel and other tools back to the cabin, I felt a delicious sense of accomplishment. Alone under the descending snow, surrounded by stillness, with no one to tell me that what I had done was dumb or smart, crazy or necessary. Far away, politicians were positioning and pontificating, trying to elbow their candidate into the presidency. My prairie would not change the world, but it would, I hoped, heal a little patch of damaged earth.

The Invasions

Many good times were still to come. We continued to manage the land to the best of our ability, mowing and burning and seeding, although finding the kind of experienced help we needed—and we did need help—was always a problem. We enjoyed many days and weekends at the new cabin with grandchildren, with friends, or alone. We hosted many groups for walks and picnics. And yet, our visits began to take on a feeling of denouement. Physical limitations were beginning to plague us. My bothersome knee had to be replaced. We tired more easily. Climbing up to the pine relict became more and more difficult.

We were fortunate to find a teenager with some background in restoration work, and he agreed to come on an hourly basis. He proved to be a willing worker and quick to learn. So when he suggested that his brother was available to help as well, we agreed. And for a while, they worked diligently clearing brush and bramble from the hill behind the cabin, in preparation for establishing the oak savanna.

That September of 2000, it did seem that we had solved most of our problems. We were settling in to the new cabin, moving in the various books and other items that had been stored in the tractor shed. My notes in the journal were cheerful and full of accomplishments:

September 8: This morning a way big fog obscures the
valley . . . I go to tractor shed to retrieve my Peterson Field
Guides. As I start lifting them out of a box of New Yorkers,
out pops a field mouse. At the bottom of the box, where
there's a safe space amongst the books, they'd built themselves a comfy haven, nestled in the shredded pages of Agatha
Christie and Garrison Keillor! Four more mice emerge as I
salvage gnawed books. Fortunately the Peterson Field Guides
were fine, if a little mildewed and probably mouse-peed!

September 14: How can I concentrate on writing when the
birds keep distracting me? After a drizzly night, everything
is bright and fresh. Hummingbirds swarm, finches attack the
finch feeder. Only the birds . . . the quiet . . . and the slow rising mist. A cardinal! The first one I've seen this fall. It sits on
a branch of poplar and observes the twittery finches. Blue jay
very noisy! Nuthatches and phoebes, and a woodpecker off
somewhere, knocking.

David and Shelley brought out a friend who was a renowned
bird expert, and just by hearing their songs he identified many
more birds than we were able to—about thirty, in addition to the
common ones we knew!

The years went by, as the journal recorded lists of chores, lists
of good plants and invasives, and the changes that occurred with
each season, each year. A naturalist friend and I fenced four test
plots—hillside and bottomland—and recorded each species over
the course of several years to document changes.

I attended workshops, made more lists. We assisted other
landowners in burning and tending their land; we bought a new
tractor. A friend put a small solar panel on the cabin roof, which
meant we had a limited but welcome power source.

The young man who had been helping us for several years moved to Florida, leaving his less reliable brother behind. The brother, whom we will call Jim, had a habit of making poor decisions, so we told him we no longer needed his help. After his departure, we tried out several other helpers, with some success.

Several times that spring when we came out for our usual work weekend, we noticed a few things out of place in the cabin. Then we discovered cigarette butts on the ground near the cabin. Since we had both given up smoking years before, these caught our attention. Probably one of the helpers, we surmised. The cabin was built with heavy wooden doors, and we kept it locked. The chain across the top of the driveway had a combination lock. Although whoever was working for us at the time knew the combination, we had long since ceased to worry about intruders.

One Tuesday in April I came out alone to do some seeding of the cleared back hill, where we were still working on the oak savanna. Everything was going wrong that day. Cowbirds were attacking the bird feeder. I was irritated by a new crop of emerging lady beetles and by the burdock coming up in the creek bed.

Then the sky darkened ominously, and fat raindrops splattered the deck. The siren sounded at noon, and I paced from window to window, peering for funnel clouds. When I looked for the radio to check for weather warnings, it was nowhere to be seen. Moreover, the cell phone was dead. It was chilly inside, and I reached for one of Laird's old shirts, hanging on a hook in the stairway, and was surprised to find a pack of cigarettes in the pocket. I tried to convince myself that perhaps the deer hunters had been out; they occasionally came out to check the cabin and the deer herd, but not often in the spring, and they always checked with us first. All in all, I was uneasy. There was nothing to be done, except wait for the sky to clear, lock up, and head for home.

I told Laird about the cigarettes in the shirt pocket and the spent bullets I'd found on the grass outside. He called the sheriff, who visited and did an initial search and fingerprinting but couldn't do much more at the time. We worried some, but we were in the midst of preparing our home on the west side of Madison to put up for sale. We had a lot of other things on our minds, and we hoped this worry would just go away.

And then one day we came out to discover that the place had obviously been used for a large party. Wet towels littered the bathroom floor, bedding was strewn around, upstairs and down, and the floor was wet.

We called the generator repairman, who had been there the day before, and asked whether he'd seen anyone. He said a bunch of teens, several girls and several boys, were just leaving when he arrived, and it looked like they had spent the night. The repairman described one of the boys, who said he worked for us and had permission to use the cabin. Sure enough, the description fit our former employee, the hapless Jim, who of course still knew the combination of the gate lock and also where we had foolishly continued to hide the cabin key.

I called the sheriff again, this time with the name of the suspect. The sheriff called Jim and also his father and threatened him with arrest if another break-in should ever occur. Then Jim called us and yelled and swore at me, shouting that he deserved to use the place for all the work he'd done!

On another weekend when we were at the cabin with our two young grandchildren, all of us decided to sleep on the deck. We had settled into hammocks and mattresses, and Laird and the kids were asleep, when I saw lights coming down the driveway and heard gravel crunching under wheels. I jumped up and yelled to Laird to get the phone, but the vehicle turned around and roared off up the hill. I suspected it was some of the former gang, who noticed that the chain was off the driveway and hoped to get in on a party. I felt chilled, shaken, invaded. It was difficult to get to sleep that night, and the whole episode left scars on my imagination.

Not long after, we did find two reliable and experienced land managers, who loved the valley and did regular burns for a number of years. But I never again felt perfectly safe in my secret garden.

Decision Time

Several land conservancies contacted us in 2011 about putting easements on the land. Since it was time to think about what would happen to the land after we were gone, we hosted a tour and picnic for our land stewardship group, the OWLS, and invited the director of the Driftless Area Land Conservancy, Dave Clutter, to talk about easements and land trusts and other long-term planning opportunities. It was a beautiful sunny day, and the prairie was in Technicolor glory. More Turk's-cap lilies were in bloom than we'd ever had before! Many of the attendees climbed up to the pine relict, while I walked another group out to one of the daisy meadows to see what burning had done for that area.

We still kept records of our burns and other labors, but too often the journal entries mentioned that the generator wouldn't work or that the tractor had broken down. Or both. Too often, mixed in with our delight and appreciation were discouraging notes on failures. One such entry noted our despair when garlic mustard, devilishly hard to get rid of, made its presence known.

In addition, since retiring, we'd discovered the joy we shared in travel, and we took many trips in this country and abroad. With three married sons settled in distant places and new grandchildren arriving regularly, we also needed to check in for grandparent duty. We started to skimp on our chores at the valley, and the neglect showed.

In fall of 2006, we moved from our home on the west side of Madison to a condo in Middleton by the Pheasant Branch Conservancy, where we volunteered to share our experience with prairie management. We walked the trails and reveled in our view across the three hundred acres of marsh and oak woods—with no personal responsibility!

Gradually our visits to the cabin at the valley decreased. We still enjoyed picnics and occasional sleepovers, but we had to recognize that the time had come to relinquish the responsibility, and we started to talk seriously about our options. We had mistakenly thought that among our siblings and offspring, someone would pick up our enthusiasm and continue our quest. But either they lived too far away, or they were simply not interested.

In 2014, one of the people we'd worked with at the DNR gave us a call, asking if we would be willing to meet with a group from the agency and talk about our plans for the future of the land. Four representatives, including a lawyer and real estate specialist, came to our house in Middleton and presented us with an offer to buy the entire 115 acres.

I asked them what would happen to the cabin, knowing that the DNR didn't like to own buildings because of the liability. Typically, they burned them down. Thinking about our lovely cabin coming to this brutal end broke my heart.

They laid out another option, called a Life Estate. Under this plan, they would buy the land, and we could retain the cabin and five acres for our use for as long as we wished or until we died. It could not be passed along to heirs. The rest of the land would be added to the adjacent parcels that they had been able to buy over the years, and the total—one thousand acres—would become the Ridgeway Pines State Natural Area, open to the public for hiking and hunting. The DNR would manage it, freeing us of the responsibility. I couldn't help thinking back to our meeting with

Mark Martin of the DNR some twenty-five years before, when he first described their aspirations.

We had some time to think it over and to discuss the proposal with Laird's siblings. Since their involvement with the property had been minimal for some time, they were agreeable. Another possibility, of course, was to sell the property on the open market. But we would have no guarantee that the land would be taken care of. No other option offered the advantages of the Life Estate offered by the DNR.

It was a difficult decision, letting go of the land we had worked on for so long and loved so deeply. Ultimately, and not without a sense of loss, we chose the Life Estate. This resolution would still allow us access to the cabin and our own five acres for the rest of our lives, as well as the opportunity to visit the new state natural area beyond our own valley. And we could still sit on the deck and watch the prairie bloom.

Epilogue

From the journal, August 31, 2008

When you have a cabin on 115 acres, with no handyman or friendly neighbor farmer, you have work—lots of hard, physical work. Friends tell you how lucky you are to have the cabin as a getaway, to write undisturbed. I try to explain to them that it is considerably harder to write at the valley than it is at home!

I wake early, with the birds. We sleep out on the deck to take advantage of every sight, sound, and smell. We love the way the air seems to pool on our skin like a cold hand. We've discovered flannel sheets and hooded sweatshirts, and we brave temperatures down to freezing.

I would like to write. I would like to describe the smell of the new wood inside the cabin, rich and resinous. I would like to luxuriate in the silence, punctuated only by birdsong, and let my eyes watch the distance change in subtle shades as the day takes hold, nudging us onward. When the sun slides above the east ridge, there will be a sudden streaming of gold, down across the pines, brightening the foliage, pooling in the prairie. Fortunately I can still contemplate this glory.

The morning continues to lighten; a swath of rosy light appears above the nearest pine bluff. A light breeze foretells a fine day. The hummingbird roars up to the feeder and dips his head twenty-two times to drink nectar. The finch feeder on the poplar is alive with yellow finches, a pair of indigo buntings, a grosbeak, and a couple of chipping sparrows.

Laird sleeps on beside me while I ponder which area of honeysuckle to attack. Our five acres still require attention. Behind the cabin on the steep, new savanna area that we see out the kitchen window would be a good target. I'd like to be able to clear the path up to the top, from where we could watch the sunset, and I make a mental note to get a bench up there.

I think back over the years, and the work, and the successes and failures. A hundred-plus acres requires a couple of sturdy, hardworking young guys with chain saws, not these two aging retirees who committed themselves to this land and sometimes got discouraged. I hope that the Department of Natural Resources will tend the valley as assiduously as we did.

We remember how the days reeled out, when we tramped and cut and chopped and sawed, till we were sweaty, muddy, and aching in the knees and back. But strangely enough, it was a good feeling.

"Next time," I used to say to Laird, "we'll just take it easy and read all day." He would laugh, and his laugh was like a resigned sigh. We would be slumped in canvas chairs on the wide front deck viewing our wondrous valley and admiring the colors, the distance, the changing gold and rose light of evening. A doe and three fawns would go tiptoeing toward the stream. We were probably drinking a gin and tonic, snacking on crackers and cheese.

"My God, we're lucky!" one of us would always say.

Acknowledgments

During the thirty years Laird and I reveled and labored in our Wisconsin valley, we enjoyed the company and assistance of many friends and neighbors and benefited from the knowledge and advice of innumerable specialists.

Foremost among these would have to be our indomitable cousins David and Shelley Hamel, who encouraged and participated in all our early ventures. These included identifying plants, managing prairie burns, annihilating honeysuckle, tending the bees, and repairing anything mechanical. Other stalwart helpers included Warren and Sharon Gaskill, Harriet Irwin, Jeff Lange and his crew, Paul Haskew, Nancy Braker, Ulrich Sielaff, Dave and Nan Cheney, Greg D'Alessio, and Owen, Meg, Jason, and Evan Marshall. Burn crews included Dave and Ned Liebl, Dotty Ballantine, Frank Sandner and Caroline Beckett, and Jim Ziegler and Sue Knapp. We welcomed other advice and assistance from Mary Trewartha, Tom and Kathie Brock, Gigi LaBudde, Jim Drescher, and Hugh Iltis.

We benefited tremendously from the expertise of many DNR specialists, including Rich Henderson, who managed our first burns, Bob Reed, botanist, and foresters Jim Witter, Tom Hill, Brad Hutnick, Scott Lancaster, John Nielson, Mike Wojcik, Stefanie Brouwer, and Mark Martin. Fred Clarke assisted in clearing and cutting.

A visit of members from the Nature Conservancy, including Fan Taylor, Peg and Jim Watrous, Katherine and Joe Bradley, and

Liza and Dick Bardwell, honored us with a plaque that designated the valley as a state natural area.

We are ever grateful to Don Richards for his design of the new cabin and to Rick Hanson for building it beautifully!

Dave Clutter and the Driftless Area Land Conservancy counseled us on easements. And to the dozens of others—too many to name!—who shared picnics and long walks, brought food, planted trees, and were generous in their admiration and encouragement, we are grateful to all!

About the Author

After retiring from corporate and non-profit communications positions, Alice D'Alessio began writing poetry and has published four books. *A Blessing of Trees* was awarded the Posner Prize from the Council for Wisconsin Writers, and *Days We Are Given* won first place and publication from Earth's Daughters. Her latest book, *Conversations with Thoreau*, was published by Parallel Press. She has taught workshops at the Green Lake Conference Center and at The Clearing Folk School in Ellison Bay, Wisconsin.

PHOTO BY AMY STOCKLEIN